Concerto for Body and Soul

Other New London Librarium Titles
by Rubem Alves

The Best Chronicles of Rubem Alves

Tender Returns

*Art of Love: Paintings by Colleen Hennessy,
Thoughts from Rubem Alves*

*Pensamentos:
Brief Bits of Wisdom from Rubem Alves*

Concerto for Body and Soul

Rubem Alves

Translated by
Glenn Alan Cheney

New London Librarium

Concerto for Body and Soul
by Rubem Alves
Translated by Glenn Alan Cheney

Original Title: *Concerto para Corpo e Alma*
Original Publisher: Editora Papirus

Copyright © 2019 Glenn Alan Cheney

Published by
New London Librarium
Hanover, CT 06350
NLLibrarium.com

All rights reserved. No part of this book may be reproduced in any medium whatsoever without the express permission of the publisher or copyright holder.

ISBNs
Paperback: 978-1-947074-40-8
Hardcover: 978-1-947074-39-2
eBook: 978-1-947074-41-5

Contents

I
Andante Grazioso

On Simplicity and Wisdom : *9*
From Addition to Subtraction : *17*
Beauty-Sadness : *24*

II
Languido

Who Am I? : *33*
On Violins and Fiddles : *41*

III
Espressivo, Delicato

The Boy and the Enchanted Butterfly : *51*
All Because of a Look : *59*
The Stepmother's Eyes : *66*

IV
Andante Con Espressione

Barbecues : *75*
Soups : *82*
Rice and Beans, Ground Beef and Tomato : *88*

V
Sincopado
On Crime and Intelligence : *99*
The Hyena Invasion : *106*
Leaf-Cutters and Bandits : *114*
The Fire Is Coming... : *122*

VI
Adagio Lamentoso
Leandro : *133*
Magnolias and Jabuticabas : *141*
A Blue Sky Immensely Nearby : *148*
To Guido, with Affection : *155*
Arrival and Departure : *162*
A Unique Moment : *169*

VII
Presto-Allegro Assai
I Am Going to Plant a Tree : *177*
Bovine Wisdom : *185*
On Optimism and Hope : 192

Acknowledgements : *201*
Rubem Alves : *202*
Glenn Alan Cheney : *203*
New London Librarium : *205*

I
Andante Grazioso

in the background,
Sonata in A major
by W.A. Mozart

On Simplicity and Wisdom

They asked me to write on simplicity and wisdom. I accepted the invitation happily, knowing that, for that request to be made, I would have to be old.

Youth and adults know little about the meaning of simplicity. The youth are birds that fly by morning. Their flights are arrows in all directions. Their eyes are fascinated by ten thousand things. They want them all, but none of them give the young rest. Youth is always ready to fly again. Their world is the world of multiplicity. They love it because in their minds, multiplicity is a space of freedom. With adults, the opposite happens. For them, multiplicity is a spell that imprisons, a trap they fall into. They hate multiplicity, but they don't know how to free themselves. If, for the young, multiplicity is called freedom, for adults, multiplicity has the name of duty. Adults are captured birds in cages of duty. Every morning, ten thousand things await them with their orders (for this, there are agendas where the ten thousand things write their orders!). If they are not obeyed, there will be penalties.

At dusk, when night draws near, the flight of birds is different. In no way does it look like their flight in the morning. Have you ever watched the flight of pigeons at the end of day? They all fly in one direction. They go back home, back to their nests. Birds at dusk are simple. Simplicity is this: when the heart seeks just one thing.

Jesus told parables about simplicity. He spoke about a man who possessed many jewels, though none of them made him happy. But one day he found a jewel, dazzling and unique, and fell in love with it. So he then made a deal that brought him happiness. He sold the many and bought the one.

In multiplicity we lose. We ignore our desire. We act in fascination with the seduction of ten thousand things. It happens that, as the second poem of the Tao Te Ching says, "The ten thousand things appear and disappear without stopping." The path to multiplicity is a path without rest. Each point of arrival is a point of departure. Every meeting is a good-bye. It's a path where there is no house or nest. The last of the temptations that the Devil tried with the Son of God was the temptation of multiplicity: "The Devil took him to a high mountain, showed him the kingdoms of the world and its glory, and said unto him: "All this I give you if you fall down and worship me." But what multiplicity does is shatter the heart. The heart that pursues the "many" is a fragmented heart, a heart without rest. The word of Jesus: "What is it worth to gain the whole world and ruin life?" (Matthew 16:26)

The path of science and of learning is the path of multiplicity. A sacred writer warns: "Of making books there is no end, and much study is wearisome to the flesh." (Ecclesiastes 12:12). There is no end to the things that can be known and understood. The world of knowledge is a world of sums without end. It is a path without rest for the soul. There is no knowledge before which the heart can say: "I have finally arrived home." Knowledge isn't home. In the best hypothesis, it is bricks with which to build a house. But the bricks themselves, know nothing about a house. The bricks belong to multiplicity. The house belongs to simplicity: a single thing.

Says the *Tao Te Ching*: "In the search for knowledge, something is added each day. In the search for wisdom, each day something is subtracted."

Says T.S. Eliot: "Where is the wisdom we lose in knowledge?"

Says Manoel de Barros: "Whoever accumulates a lot of information loses the wandering of guessing. The wise one is the one who guesses."

Wisdom is the art of savoring. On wisdom, Nietzsche said: "The Greek word is linked, etymologically, to *sapio*, I savor; *sapiens*, the savorer; *sisyphus*, the man of the most perfect taste." Wisdom is, therefore, the art of savoring, distinguishing, discerning. The man of knowledge, in the face of multiplicity, "plunges into every thing that it is possible to learn, in the blind eagerness of wanting to know at any price." But the wise one is in search of "things worthy of being known."

Imagine a buffet. On the table, an enormous multiplicity, an infinitude of dishes. The man of learning, fascinated with the dishes, throws himself at them. He wants to eat it all. The wise one, on the other hand, stops and asks his body: "In all this multiplicity, which is the dish that will give you the most pleasure and joy?" And then, after meditating on it, he chooses one…

Wisdom is the art of recognizing and savoring joy. We are born into joy. Bachelard says that the entire universe is destined to happiness.

Vinicius de Morães wrote a beautiful poem with the title *Remain*…Already old, having walked the world of multiplicity, he looked back and saw what remained—what was worthwhile. "What remains is this heart, burning like a candle in a cathedral in ruins…" "What remains is the capacity for tenderness…" "What's left is this old respect for the night…" "What's left is this desire to cry before beauty…" And so goes Vinicius, counting the experiences that gave him joy. They were what was left.

The things that remain survive in a place in the soul called longing. Longing is the pocket where the soul keeps that which it tasted and approved. The approved were the experiences that gave joy. What was worthwhile is destined to eternity. Longing is the face of eternity reflected in the river of time. This is why we need gods, so that the river of time is circular: "Cast your bread upon the waters, for after many days thou shalt find it…" We pray that that which was lost in the past be returned to us in the future. I think God doesn't mind if we call it the Eternal Return—for that is all we ask of him, that the longed-for be returned.

I wander through the caverns of my memory. There are many wonderful things: scenes, places, some heavenly, others strange and curious, trips, events that mark the time of my life, meetings with notable people. But these memories, despite their size, don't do anything for me. I feel no desire to cry. I feel no desire to return.

So I consult my pocket of longing. There I find pieces of my body, pieces of joy. I look carefully, and nothing I find shined out in the world of multiplicity. They are little things that weren't even noticed by other people: scenes, paintings: a young son launching a kite on the beach; a night of insomnia and fear in a dark room, and in the middle of the darkness the voice of a son saying, "Daddy, I really like you"; a daughter playing with a puppy now dead (I cried a lot over her, Flora); a boy riding a horse before sunrise in a field perfumed with ripe hay; an old man smoking a pipe, contemplating the rain that fell on plants, saying, "See how grateful they are!" Friends. Memories of poems, of stories, of songs.

Guimarães Rosa said "happiness only in rare moments of distraction…" Correct. It comes when it isn't expected, in places unimagined. Jesus said: "It's like the wind: it blows where it wants, you don't know where it comes from or where it goes…" Wisdom is the art of tasting and joy, when it comes. But this art is mastered only by those who have the grace of simplicity. Because joy lives only in simple things.

From Addition to Subtraction

At the end of the year, for reasons unrelated to my will, my body goes through a metamorphosis. I become different. I feel like its software is changing.

Software refers to the program, the logic a computer works with. During the year, my body is driven by a software that only knows the logic of "addition." I add up all the time. I add on things. I don't throw anything away. I make annotations. I don't forget. Memory is also a way of adding up.

There are two reasons that lead me to add up. The first is love. I save because I love. That's the case of letters that arrive. They are letters from people who wish me well. They tell me good things that make me happy. Love can remain without response. The right thing to do would be to answer the letters at the exact moment I read them and become happy. But life has urgencies greater than those of love. The letters go without answer. So my solution is to add them up in piles, to be answered in the future. But what was true on one day is true for them all. The piles go on growing. The year comes to an end. The pile is enormous. The letters remain unanswered.

The second reason is utility. It's possible that the object in my hands, of dubious utility, may have some use in the future. So, availing myself of the benefit of the doubt, I save it. At the end of the year, my drawers are a mess that I don't understand, messes stupid with an unbelievable quantity of varied objects that, out of shame, I am not going to list.

But now, as year comes to an end...

(End? Evidently referring to man's illusion that the means of marking time represents the beating of the heart of the universe—thus the festivities, the champaign, the feasting. We really believe that a certain time is agonizing: an evil old man whose death is toasted with parties. Now another time arrives, newly born, blank pages without memory, accounts zeroed out, and everything will change. It is only this childish belief that explains the enormous brouhaha made because of a change of calendars—because that's all that happens. An old calendar into the trash, a new calendar on the wall. The stars, time keepers, ignore it all and continue to watch over us with the same indifferent eyes and silences as always, to the horror of Pascal...)

...but, as I was saying, now, as the year ends, my software changes. The program that "added up" is uninstalled, and in its place, the "subtraction" program begins to run. The "add up" program is a nasty conjuration: the more it accumulates, the heavier it gets. We lose lightness. Walking around becomes difficult. There's too much fat and muscle. The body sinks from too much weight. It's the devil who adds up. The "subtraction" program is the opposite. It breaks the add-up spell. We lose weight, become light, shed scales. Scabs peel off. The body loses bulk and grows wings. "Adding up" makes us grow old. "Subtraction" returns us to childhood. The devil adds up: he has an implacable accounting that does not forget. God subtracts. He has no accounting. Every forgiving is a forgetting.

The piles of letters: until a few days ago, possessed by the logic of adding up, I looked at them and became anguished. They were telling me there was a duty to fulfill. Love letters must be answered. The pile of letters was telling me that I was not fulfilling my duty. But, all of a sudden, the logic of adding up went away, and the logic of subtraction took its place. Álvaro de Campos agrees.

> *Ah! The freshness of not fulfilling a duty! What a refuge, to not be worthy of trust! I breathe better now...*
> *I am free, contrary to clothed and organized society. I am naked, and I dive into the water of my imagination...*

So I give myself to the grace of "subtraction." With the eyes of someone saying good-bye, I looked at the letters that the sense of duty was obliging me to answer. I am going to deliver them to forgetting. I am going to subtract them from the place they occupy. They will no longer remain there, in front of me like a liability. I tenderly take them in my hands. I will say good-bye to each of them. I re-read passages, and I smile, happy once again. I ask forgiveness from the friends who wrote to me. The letters will remain without written response, though the response of my heart has very much been given in the joy they created in me. This does not mean a lack of love. It's that I am not the Lord of Time. I need more time than I have. Not even love can deal with it. It is from this impotence of love in the face of time that art is born.

Tempus fugit—this Latin phrase is engraved on a wooden plaque on the door of my office. *Time flies.* I saw the phrase, the first time, on one of those antique clocks that toll every quarter hour, monotonously repeating: *tempus fugit...tempus fugit.* A Biblical psalm says: "Teach us to number our days that we may gain a heart of wisdom." Wisdom begins when we learn to tell time. Those who tell time know that time does not add up, it only subtracts. And that's why the letters will have to go without response. My friends will understand. They will forgive. If they don't forgive, it's because they weren't my friends. I am going to start the year off very light, without letters to answer. In the place where they are now will be the delicious emptiness on the varnished surface of wood, a space that isn't telling me something.

I look at the rest of the house. The logic of subtraction has its work cut out for it. I rummage through drawers, shelves, boxes, closets, in search of things that have accumulated during the year. Before each thing I ask two questions. First: Do I love it? If the answer is positive, the decision is made. Things that are loved must remain. If the answer is negative, I ask a second question: Is it useful? If the answer is negative again, the sentence is rendered: It will have to vacate the space. My house, for the new time, must be full of emptiness.

Álvaro de Campos, euphoric with the freedom of not fulfilling duties, ends by saying, "I am naked, and I dive into the water of my imagination."

Water is the great power of subtraction. Wherever it passes, it cleans. So I imagined a ritual for the celebration, not of the dubious passing of the year but of the body's joyous return to childhood—the dive into the waters. The waters have the power of subtracting, from the body and the soul, the heavy things that the passage of time built up in them. The waters carry us to forgetting. They wash the aged body, and the body returns to being a child.

A dive into the waters: sea water, rain water, river water, lake water, the water of a waterfall, a shower, a bathtub, a swimming pool, a squirt, any water—or, if for some reason these dives are not possible, a *dive into the water of the imagination*.

It isn't by chance that the religious symbol for metamorphosis is a sinking into water. Rising from the water, the old person who went down is dead, and in the person's place a child arises with a new name. I am going to think of a new name for myself.

Concerto for Body and Soul

Beauty-Sadness

I've been going around rather sad. Some of my friends have noticed and started worrying. I want to calm them. I am, in fact, sick. But it isn't a serious sickness. I suffer from beauty. It isn't by accident that, in Portuguese, beauty (*beleza*) rhymes with sadness (*tristeza*). Albert Camus said that beauty is intolerable. Spanish Jewish poet Rafael Consinos-Asséns asked God that there not be so much beauty. Vincius De Morães confessed that beauty made him want to cry. Adélia Prado agrees, saying that the beautiful fills her eyes with water. And Cecília Meireles, the one who "wanted to teach the sands and ice about spring," described herself as "one who suffered from beauty." That's it: I, too, suffer from beauty.

Beauty produces in me a mild sadness. I'm not saying it should be cured. If I cured it, if I became kind of happy, I would stop being who I am. My sadness is as much a part of me as the color of my eyes, the beating of my heart, my hands. Without my sadness, I would be crippled. I think I might even stop writing. Because my writing is a musical counterbalance to my sadness. Alberto Caseiro felt that way, too:

> *But I become sad like a sunset*
> *when it turns cold on the plain*
> *and feel the night coming on*
> *like a butterfly at the window.*
> *But my sadness is quietness*
> *because it is natural and just*
> *and is what it should be in my soul…*
> *Once in a a while it is necessary to be unhappy*
> *in order to be natural.*

Nietzsche, when still very young, said that in art, "a brilliant image of clouds and sky seems mirrored in the black lake of sadness." There is no art without sadness. The beauty of art counterbalances the sadness of life. Psychiatrists and jolly people want to cure sadness. They prescribe pills and tell jokes. But I think prescription is something else. One must become friends with sadness. One who befriends sadness becomes more beautiful.

I am listening to Bach at this moment. It's the music of Bach that's to blame for my sadness. Music is spellbinding. Bach was a spellbinder. Music, without a single word, without any way for reason to defend itself, goes inside the body and goes to the bottom of the soul. Hearing music, I become defenseless. My critical consciousness is dead. The beauty leaves no place for thoughts. Anything I think will be a noise that ruins the beauty. I feel sorry for music critics. They are obliged, by profession, to think while they listen. And the thought robs them of the possibility of trance. The song has entered every part of my body. I am in ecstasy, forgetting everything else. To hell with you, Descartes, with your "I think therefore I am." I say, "I am possessed by music, therefore I am."

Speleology is the science of caverns. I studied a speleology dedicated to exploring the caverns of the soul. The soul is a maze of caverns lit by a light that infiltrates through narrow cracks, caverns that grow ever deeper and darker. Outside is the sunlit world, "a great fair, all tents and street performers" (Fernando Pessoa), a lot of people, yackety-yack, shouting, gossip, laughter, everybody talking, nobody listening, everybody exchanging words they know, and everybody wearing smiling masks. The entrance to the cavern is hidden by vegetation. Few find it. Few have the courage to enter. Inside, everything is different. The spaces shaped by the millennia call for few words. Voices turn into whispers. But eyes grow. And so we go descending, deeper and deeper, until we find ourselves. There is solitude and silence. The truth of the soul is beyond words. It cannot be spoken.

After a long descent, we arrive at the bottom of the cavern. There's a lake down there, there for many millennia, a lake of absolute blue. (It's in the city of Bonito, in the Brazilian state of Mato Grosso do Sul.) The bottom of the soul is a lake. An enchanted lake. From it arises a melody. At the absolute bottom of the soul, there where the solitude is total, there where words cease—music is heard. Fernando Pessoa knew that and said so in a verse: "... and the melody that wasn't, if now I remember it, makes me cry." The melody that wasn't makes us remember the beauty that we lost. Narcissus saw his beauty reflected in the surface of the lake. In music our beauty appears as a sonorous entity. Hearing music, we turn into music. I am the music of Bach that I am hearing. It's an ephemeral joy. Because, contrary to painting and sculpture, music happens in time—and the beauty runs through the body like water. A joy felt, soon to be lost. Thus the sadness of music, and my sadness.

My sadness is provoked by a CD, the same one I'm listening to. The music of the Grupo Corpo. Grupo Corpo is a dance company. It is not possible to describe it. I only know that, in the few times I've seen it, I became possessed. My body refused to simply see the show. It wanted to embrace what it saw and heard. Music is like that: it doesn't want to be just heard. It wants to possess bodies, transform itself into life, turn into flesh. "...and Music became flesh..."

It's a different Bach, transformed by the group Uakti, which specializes in strange instruments and unknown sounds. At this precise moment, the chorale begins: "Come sweet death. Come blessed rest. Come, take me to joy, for I am tired of the world. Come, I await you. Come soon and take me. Close my eyes. Come, blessed rest." I have already heard this chorale many time, and I actually got to play it on the organ. But never the way I heard it played by Uakti. They produced a strange, metallic sound on an instrument that Bach did not know. Could it be, by chance, a *berimbau* played by a bow? It's so sad.

But soon the sadness ceases and turns into joy, the delicious *Courante*, a ternary rhythm, a waltz, an urge to dance followed by the aria of a soprano from the chorale *Jesu, Joy of Man's Desiring*, accompanied by the melodic movement of the prelude of the First Suite for Cello.

And here I remain, hearing this Bach do-si-do without tiring. And I am hearing "the melody that wasn't." That's why I cry and grow sad. But it isn't a sadness of sadness, it's a sadness of so much beauty that it's too much for me.

But it's also a sadness that is sadness. There is a great solitude down at the bottom, where the lake is blue and the melody is heard. I am alone. No one can arrive where I am. At the bottom of the soul the solitude is total.

My sadness is mild and good. Don't worry about me. Adélia said, "The one who can deal with sadness is the one who has not lost happiness." As long as I hear Bach, I am safe.

II
Languido

accompanied by the Russian song
Black Eyes

Who Am I?

Who am I?
I know I am many. Who taught me this was an old Demon, the same who taught Jesus psychology. When Jesus asked him, "What is your name?" he responded, in a cross between truth and joshing, "My name is Legion because we are." What a crazy thing: The "I," singular in grammar, plural in psychology.

I am many. One has the impression that it is dealing with the same person because the body is the same. In fact the body is one. The "I's" who live within it are many.

We know they are many because of the music that each one plays. The words don't matter. The words could even be the same. What makes the difference is the music. Each "I" plays a different song, with different instruments: oboe, violin, timpani, cymbals, trombone. Together they can make up an orchestra. They don't. Each "I" plays whatever pops up. As in the film *Orchestra Rehearsal*. I forget the name of the director. Was it Fellini? It's worth seeing.

Sometimes the "I's" hate themselves. Many suicides could be explained as assassinations. One "I" doesn't like the music of the other, so it kills it. That was the case of my cousin. When we were seven years old and playing with little lead soldiers, he was making a comparative dictionary of four languages: Portuguese, English, French, and German. When he got a 98 on a test, he smacked his hand on his forehead and, devastated, said, "I failed!" The "I" who hit himself in the forehead was the "I" who could not stand to not be perfect. The "I" who took the smack on the head was the I that hadn't managed to get a

100 on the test. One day, the first "I" got tired of smacking the forehead of the second "I." He took a definitive measure. He obliged him to throw himself out a 17th floor window.

Correct Portuguese says, "I am." Singular subject, singular verb. But those who learned from Socrates, those who know themselves, know that the soul does not line up with grammar.

Albert Camus states, in his book *Man in Revolt*, that man is the only being that refuses to be what he is. This affirmation can be illustrated perfectly in a banal incident, described by Barthes in his book *Camera Lucida: Reflections on Photography*.

From the moment when I feel watched by the object of the photographic camera, everything changes. I put myself in a pose, fabricating myself into another body, metamorphosing in advance of the image.

I look at the photo. I suffer. The photograph caught me drifting. I didn't come out good. I don't recognize myself in that image. I am much better looking. I suffer even more when my friends confirm: "You came out good!" What they are saying is that I really do look that way. I complain about my own body. I refuse to be like that. I need to be alert so they don't photograph me off guard. If I see that I'm going to be photographed, I'll assume a pose. The pose is the subtle movement I make with my body in hopes of making it coincide with the slick image that I love and which escapes me. The image I love is well outside my body. I refuse to be my unguarded image. The posing movement must coincide with it. I want to be the beautiful image.

The myth of Narcissus tells the truth about mankind. Narcissus accepted death in order to not be separated from his beautiful image—the one that, like Narcissus, lives the reality that coincides with the beloved image without needing to pose. He is ready to die. Death eternalizes the image.

The religious say that human existence justifies itself morally. God desires us to be good. I disagree. Human existence justifies itself aesthetically. We are destined to beauty. God, the Creator, first sought beauty. Paradise is the consummation of beauty. God looked at the garden and was happy. It was beautiful! In Paradise, there were no ethics or morality. There was only aesthetics. The saints the Church canonized for their goodness were driven by the desire to be found beautiful by God. Beauty generates goodness. When we feel ugly, we are possessed by envy and desires of vengeance. The envious and the vengeful are people who suffer from feeling ugly.

Beauty isn't a physical thing. It can't be photographed. It's a music that comes out of the body. In this way we are the same as poems. A poem, according to Fernando Pessoa, is words within whose interstices one hears a melody so lovely that it can make one cry. The beauty of poems isn't found in that which it is but precisely in that which is *not*: the unsaid where the music is born.

Of all the "I's," which one am I? I am the face of beauty. That's what I love—precisely that which is slick and which I try to capture in that pose! Because this "I" which I love, this is the "I" that my love chooses as my true "I." The other "I's" are intrusive, demons who inhabit me and who also say, "I." And there are still doubts about the existence of those demons! How to doubt it? If they live inside me and take hold of my body and make me ugly—bad! If, in moments when they take possession of my face, I see my image reflected in a mirror, I might well die of horror or break the mirror.

It would be good if I no longer remembered this other that I am and its deformed body. But memory does not allow. It sets before me the other face that I don't want to be. Like in the novel *The Picture of Dorian Gray*. When it does so, memory destroys the spell of the "pose." It doesn't allow me to fool myself. Alberto Caeiro knew the cruelty of memory. When I remember how something was, my eyes can't see it as it is now:

> *Recollection is a betrayal of Nature.*
> *Because the Nature of yesterday isn't Nature.*
> *What was isn't anything,*
> *and to remember isn't to see.*

Every day we are new. But memory of what was yesterday ruins the newness of being. Oh, how nice it would be if we were like birds:

> *Rather the flight of birds, which goes by and leaves no trace,*
> *Than the creature which goes by and leaves tracks on the ground.*
> *The bird goes by and forgets, which is how it should be.*
> *The creature, no longer there, hence useless,*
> *Shows it was once there, which serves no purpose.*

One knows the creature by its tracks. Memory is the tracks we leave on the ground.

Marital arguments are exercises in memory. They say they are arguing over this or that. It's a lie. They always argue over the tracks. They invoke tracks, that which I was yesterday, to destroy the lovely face I love. It doesn't help that today I am a bird. "You tell me you're a bird? But these tracks tell me that yesterday you were an ape…Your pose doesn't fool me…."

To forgive is to forget. God is forgetting. When He forgives, the tracks disappear. To forgive is to wipe away the memory of the tracks or face that was deformed yesterday.

> *I appreciate your presence only with my eyes.*
> *It's more worthwhile to see a thing always by the first time you see it.*
> *Because knowing is as if never having seen it the first time.*
> *And to never have seen it the first time is to only hear tell of it.*

"I know you..." says one to the other. "My memory says who you are. I know you—I will never see you for the first time. Your face, I know it as the sum of your tracks..." Here a love story ends because love only survives where there is the forgiveness of forgetting.

We are Narcissus. We are in search of eyes in which our beautiful image reflects. We want to be beautiful. If we are beautiful, we are good.

Rubem Alves

On Violins and Fiddles

I have enormous sympathy for those who have been victims of an error of nature. Nature's error cannot be hidden. It is visible to all who have eyes. The body is different from the bodies of "normal" people. It's not in the shape that should have been born. It belongs to that bunch of people who "fled the norm," who are "ab-normal." They are therefore classified [in Brazil] as "carriers of a deficiency," which means "to have something missing," "to have a flaw."[1] From the Latin *de + facere*, in English, *away from + do*, one who does not manage to do. An imperfect body. An error of nature.

---

[1] In Brazil, where Rubem Alves lived, "portador de deficiência" is the legal and respectful term for people with disabilities.

Concerto for Body and Soul

The religious look for divine reasons to explain events—as if that "deficient" body were the product of a decision of God. When I say body, I am including therein intelligence, since intelligence is the wings that the body created to be able to fly. Such thoughts save them when, in the depths of their pain, looking at their child's different body, or looking at their own body, they ask the same terrible and inevitable question: "Why? Why me? Why was I chosen? Why am I not like the rest?" And then comes the sensation of a grand injustice—which is followed by a feeling of revulsion with life. I feel very sorry for these people. First, for the suffering caused by the difference itself. Second, because their God is very cruel. He, God, being all-powerful, could have impeded what happened. But he didn't impede. If he didn't impede it's because He didn't want to. My suffering, or the suffering of my child, is a product of God's desire. God is happy with my suffering. Religiously they are repeating the horrendous belief: "It is God's will." Well, how to love such a God, so indifferent to human suffering? They don't take into consideration that, if all things are the result of the will of God, in our universe there would only be beauty and goodness, since God is beauty and goodness. Up until now God is being born, the universe is in birth pangs, and what exists is a great symphony of groaning, since the Holy Spirit singing a duet with all those who have been marked by indifference (Romans 8:22-23).

There's the suffering of the body itself: pains, incapacities, limitations.

But there's a terrible pain in the looks of other people. If there were no looks, if all were blind, then the difference wouldn't hurt so much. Looks hurt because the startled eyes of others are marked with the stigma-curse: "You are different."

Equality is something everyone desires. Children want to be equals. Thus the importance of having the toy that everyone else has. The girl who didn't have a Barbie was crippled, excluded from conversations about toys, about trades. The child who didn't have the "little electronic animal" was a child with a deficiency. "How can you not have the little electronic animal if all the kids have a little animal?" The parents bought the little animal—even though they knew it was idiotic—so that their child wouldn't feel the pain of exclusion. Adolescents all wear sneakers of the same brand, T-shirts of the same designer label, do all the same things, smoke and sniff what they smoke and sniff. They use the same words, words that only they understand. And then one who speaks words in the language of parents, or who uses sneakers and T-shirts of a brand unknown. This adolescent is "different," "doesn't belong" to the group, is the "carrier of a deficiency"—in the mathematical sense where equals belong. Those who are different "don't belong." They are excluded. The different are condemned to loneliness.

The carriers of deficiencies are condemned, from the start, to loneliness. By being physically different and for not being able to do what everyone does, they are excluded from the group.

To be equal is easy. It's enough to let yourself be carried by the wave, to go on doing what everyone does. There's no need to think much or make decisions. The decisions have already been made. It's just a matter of catching the wave. Life is a big party. But the "different" are alone. No wave exists to take them away, no clique to carry them. Every movement is a battle.

The "normal" may simply say, "I am equal to everyone, therefore I am." Their equality defines their being. But "carriers of deficiencies" have to make an additional: *Pugno, ergo sum* — I struggle, therefore I am. Many, without the courage to confront their loneliness, give up living and are destroyed. The ones that accept the challenge, however, transform themselves into warriors.

There are gardens made by retail purchases. All you have to do is buy the plants at a nursery or a store. The plants are produced in a series, in land scientifically prepared. They are beautiful gardens, made with plants produced in series, all the same. But there are gardens of solitudes that bloom among rocks. In the town of Pocinhos, the Pedra Blanca — White Rock — dominates over the valley. It's a hike of several hours through the woods before it opens on the naked, volcanic rock sculpted by millennia of water and wind. People climb up, and all of a sudden, a garden appears—orchids, bromeliads, flowers, mosses—all in an immense solitude.

People are like that, too. Some are gardens produced in series. They seem different, but they are all the same. Whoever wants one calls a landscaper. And there are those that no landscaper knows how to make. With a beauty all their own, they sprout from brute volcanic rock,

In the city of Campinas, in the state of São Paulo, the Center for Independent Life was founded. It is a non-governmental organization with the mission of bringing together people who are carriers of deficiencies. The Philosophy of Independent Life arose in the United States in the 1970s. It was created by people with serious disabilities, the majority of them coming out of the war in Vietnam. It's objective is to encourage people with disabilities to lead their lives independently, without fear and without shame: to make gardens sprout in brute rock. I am reminded of my friend Roberto, a Brazilian in the United States. With the lower half of his body paralyzed by polio, he lived alone, drove a car, worked, loved, and always present, in his wheelchair, in the rallies against the war. If I am not mistaken, he was even arrested. He visited us often. It was easy because we lived on the ground floor. Later, we moved to the third story of a building without elevators. I said to Roberto, "What a shame! Now that we are on the third floor, it's going to be hard for you!" He looked at me, laughed, and said, "You seem strong enough to carry me up to the third floor!" And so it was. He got up on my shoulders, and I carried him, panting, up the stairs...

I had a friend named Gramani. He was a fiddle player. A fiddle is a violin carrying a deficiency. There are many fine violins without deficiency that only go out of tune. In the hands of Gramani, a fiddle made of huge bamboo, deficient, played Bach. Because that's how people are...

III
Espressivo, Delicato

to the tune of
Scenes from Childhood
by R. Schumann

The Boy and the Enchanted Butterfly

The numbers tell me that much time has gone by. But memory ignores it. It's as if it happened yesterday. Eternity isn't the forever. Eternity is the time when the distant becomes near. Riobaldo[2] knew these things. "Telling is very hard," he said. "Not for the years that have already passed but for the cunning way that certain past things seesaw, bouncing around from their places. The memory of a life is stored in diverse sections. One event doesn't combine well with the others. Telling them in order, one tacked onto the next, only works for stuff of

---

[2] Riobaldo is the protagonist in João Guimarães Rosa's novel *Grande Sertão: Veredas*. Though middle-class and educated, Riobaldo joins up with bandits in the impoverished outback (*sertão*) of Bahia. As he tells the tale, Riobaldo reveals an astute wisdom in archaic, colloquials neologisms.

shallow importance. That's what I think; that's how I tell them. There are long-gone times that come much closer to us than others of recent date. All longing is a kind of old age."

That's just how I am, longing, with the long-gone times quite close to me... A five-year-old girl, my daughter, cries. She's scared. I'm going off on a trip and will spend a long time away. She doesn't want me to go. She asks me to stay, but there's nothing I can do. A story pops up. It's always like that. They arise all of a sudden, without me having thought of them, coming from somewhere I do not know... So yesterday, all of a sudden, after many years, it was told again, not to the girl but to me, with a wily and maternal smile. Maybe because this time, I was the one who was crying with the fear of longing. The story goes like this:

Once upon a time there was a Girl whose best friend was an Enchanted Bird. It was enchanted in two ways. First, because it did not live in a cage. It lived free. It came and went as it wanted. It came because it loved. Second, because whenever it returned, its feathers were different colors, colors of the place where it had flown. Once it came back with its feathers immaculately white, and it told stories of mountains covered in snow. Another time its feathers were red, and it told of deserts enflamed by the sun. Girl and Bird were so happy when they were together. But there always came a time when the Bird said, "I must leave." The girl cried and implored, "Please, don't go. I get so sad. I will miss you. I'm going to cry..." "I, will miss you, too," said the Bird. "I, too, am going to cry. But I'm going to tell you a secret. I am enchanted only because of longing. It's the sadness of longing that makes me enchanted. It's the sadness of longing that makes my feathers beautiful. If I don't go, there will be no longing. I will stop being the Enchanted Bird. You will stop loving me."

And off it went. The girl, all alone, cried. And it was during a night of longing that she had an idea. "If the Bird can't leave, it will stay. If it stays, we will always be happy. And for it not to leave, it just needs to be held in a cage."

And thus it went. The Girl bought the most beautiful cage of silver. When the Bird returned, they hugged each other, it told stories, and it went to sleep. The Girl, taking advantage of its drowsiness, put him in the cage. When the Bird awoke, it gave a shout of pain.

"Ah, Girl... What have you done? You have broken the enchantment! My feathers will become ugly, and I will forget all my stories. Without longing, love departs..."

The Girl didn't believe it. She thought the Bird would end up getting used to it.

But that's not what happened. Its feathers and crest fell out. The reds, the greens, and the blues of the feathers turned a sad gray. And silence came. The Bird stopped singing. The Girl also became sad. It wasn't the bird that she had loved. And she cried all night, thinking about what she had done to her friend...

Until she could no longer stand it. She opened the door of the cage. "You can go, Bird," she said. "Come back when you want…"

"Thank you, Girl," the Bird said. "I will go and come back when I am enchanted again. And be aware: I will become enchanted again when longing returns inside me and inside you…"

This is how the story ends: The Girl waits, preparing herself for the Bird's return. But since she didn't know where it would be coming from, all places became enchanted. It could come back from anywhere. And all the moments became enchanted. At any moment it might return. When longing squeezed her little heart, she said, "How good! My Bird is becoming enchanted again!" And so, every night she went to bed sad with longing but happy, thinking, "Who knows, tomorrow he will return…" And she dreamed with the joy of meeting again.

I told this story to my little girl, Raquel. Time passed. The Bird changed its habits. It started flying more on the wings of thought than inside an airplane. When one travels by plane, the return is more complicated. It takes time. When one travels by thought, it's different. To come back, a "Hi!" suffices, and the traveller is back.

And the Girl changed, too. The Girl—she was the one in a cage. She didn't have permission to fly. But even if she had permission, it wouldn't help. She didn't have the courage to fly. The only ones who can fly are those with the courage to face loneliness. Loneliness is terrifying. Albert Camus told me that the good trip is the one where you feel fear. We humans are strange creatures. We like to feel fear. We scale mountains, hang over abysms. We throw ourselves into empty space, trusting fragile wings. We dive into depths of the sea, surrounded by danger. Trips are the same—to be more than banal relocations in space, they have to be leaps into the unknown, with all their spine-chilling. The Girl couldn't fly because she had no wings on her body. And she had no wings in her soul. The wings of the soul are called courage. Courage isn't the absence of fear. It's going forth *despite* fear.

The Bird, distracted, always thought of the Girl as a child without wings. It didn't notice that something strange was happening. Wings were beginning to grow on her shoulders. Not the wings of a bird. No one is like a bird. They were delicate butterfly wings. Once the wings had grown, it was finally time for what had to happen sooner or later. The Girl went to the Bird and said, "I must leave."

The Bird felt like saying, "Please, don't go...." It was afraid of distance. When the Girl was nearby, it would care for her. All she had to do was grow sad, and the Bird would come be next to her. It wanted to save her from the danger, the longing, the loneliness. It wanted her to be safe. But it knew that the only safe place was inside a cage. And happiness does not exist inside cages. Butterflies live in closed cocoons only for a while. All of a sudden they depart for life, for flight, for danger, for happiness.

The script of the story changed. It had to be another story. The Enchanted Bird turned into a Boy with (a few) white hairs. On his hand sits a colorful butterfly. He contemplates it, enchanted. But he knows that at this moment, the Butterfly set on his hand is ephemeral. He watches and waits. The Butterfly is going to fly. And, sad at the parting and happy with the flight of the Butterfly, he says, "Fly! I will miss you. But I know that it is longings that make us enchanted creatures...."

All Because of a Look

The holy scripture says that in the beginning there was Paradise. A man and a woman, their bodies peacefully naked, enjoyed the happiness of the other's gaze. The eyes of the other were a caress. Paradise began with a look. Then there was a disturbance. A delicious fruit provoked an evil metamorphosis. The eyes transformed. The man and the woman began to fear each other's look. They were ashamed of their own bodies. They made precarious loincloths of fig leaves. God felt sorry for them. He understood that Paradise, because of a bad look, was definitively lost. So the Creator gave them gift of mercy — permission to live the rest of their days hidden from each other. And he even made them tunics with which to cover their bodies. Paradise was lost and the gates were closed. All because of a look.

The gates of Paradise closed. Closed was the door of the kitchen. The orders were for a certain young girl to not enter the salons of the house, which were prepared for a ball. That night, everything was to be lovely and perfect. No ugly and disheveled girl was going to perturb the moment of glory for the mother and sisters, who were so lovely. The presence of the girl in the ball rooms would cause bewildered looks, spread unease and shame and then a need for explanations. Mother and daughters did everything so that their eyes and the eyes of their guests would be spared. So the girl was to stay in the kitchen.

It wasn't the first time. She was always different. In the Disney story, she was a pretty orphan who had a fairy godmother protector who was in charge of making her beauty shine. It wasn't that way in the original story.

One time the father... What intrigues me most about these stories is the role of fathers—good men, full of love, but always distant, not noticing the suffering of the daughter and the evil of the mother. Where was Snow White's father? I think he lived inside a mirror. He was the mirror. His eyes were spellbound by his vain wife, who only thought of herself. But, all of a sudden, his eyes open. He sees his daughter. And that's when the evil stepmother turned into a witch. She couldn't stand that the father had eyes for the daughter that he didn't have for her. Jealousy always turns people into witches. And the father? Never heard from again. He disappeared into the shattered fragments of the mirror.

In another story the stepmother buries a stepdaughter. The father, an innocent fool, notices nothing. The one who takes care of the matter is the gardener. Fathers—could it be that they're fools? How to explain this, that the fathers, though having eyes, see nothing. I don't know. I don't understand.

So Cinderella's father, going off on a trip to distant lands, calls his daughters and asks them to tell him what presents they'd like him to bring. The first asks for clothes of famous fashion designers. The second requests French perfume. Cinderella, the little fool, poor thing, understanding nothing of the fame of urban vanity, driven by rustic sentiments, makes a strange request: that he, the father, bring her the first tree branch that his head bumps into. And here's what happened. Each one received the requested gifts. The girl with the broken branch took it out to a field and buried it, watered it, took care of it. The branch took, covered itself with leaves, turned into a leafy tree where birds made their nests. When the girl was sad, she came to tell the tree about her pains. The tree was her mother. For mothers are this: the place where you can cry without being ashamed.

There are many places where you can laugh: parties, bars, dinners, Disney World, with friends and with people you don't know. The laughter doesn't need to be justified. But there are few places where you can cry without feeling ashamed—and without having to put up with the twaddle of the insensitive who want to turn your crying into laughter. They don't understand. "Mother is the place where you can cry without feeling ashamed."

What a beautiful metaphor that is, for a mother: a tree. Trees are always waiting. Those who seek them out are sheltered in their shade. They are silent. They know how to listen. They're in no hurry. Under trees, thoughts calm down. They don't talk about the stupidity of men and women rushing around, always looking for the looks of others. Poor grown-ups: always prisoners of the eyes of others and the thoughts they imagine live in others. Trees don't have eyes. That's why they don't make comparisons. They don't say that this is more beautiful than that. (Cursed are school report cards! Mirrors where stepmothers look for the faces of their children! They're good for making comparisons. Report cards separate the children who go to the ball from the children who go to the cinders. It's report cards that put children into the game of comparison and envy that parents play with their children.)

In those trees live birds, the girl's friends. Little birds, symbols of fragility and innocence.

In the Disney story, everything ends well. The evil stepmother and her horrible daughters suffer the punishment of having to watch Cinderella's triumph. The original story is different. The birds, emissaries of the tree-mother, accompany the procession that follows behind Cinderella's wedding with the Prince. On the steep steps of the church, they come in quickly, and their sharp beaks perforate one of the stepmother's and the daughters' eyes. As the stepmother and daughters leave the church after the wedding, the birds come again poke out their other eyes. Vengeance is sweet. They were castrated of their most terrible organ.

The Little Prince says that "the essential is invisible to the eyes." Tiresias, the blind seer of the Oedipus myth, according to Oedipus himself, was the one who, being blind, saw things that those who could see could not see. Could it be that the stepmother and her daughters, when they became blind, turned into seers and came to see the essential? I cannot say. The story does not reveal whether the stepmother and daughters managed to see or not.

What I do know is that it is surprising how those with perfect eyes are blind. The fathers in all these stories had perfect eyes yet saw nothing. And many are the birth mothers who never see their children. What they see is, on one hand, what they wish their children were—beautiful, intelligent, charming, heroic, friendly, successful, stage characters receiving applause. And they themselves say, "I did it! I did it!"

On the other hand, they see their offspring as common children, limited, not so good-looking, not so smart, with no special charm or stage presence—just children who could be happy if their parents' eyes didn't transform them into Cinderella, the girl who slept with the cinders. When this happens, all that's left for the parents to do is pray that the birds don't come to seek revenge.

The Stepmother's Eyes

If I were intimate with the Creator, I would tell him that there's something to be done to alleviate the suffering of children. Just change their parents' eyes. In the place of their eyes, put the eyes of the grandparents. The eyes of grandparents see grandchildren in a way that's different from that of parents.

I know this from experience. When I was a young father, I looked in a hurry. My eyes ran agitatedly over ten thousand things that swirled around us. They hadn't yet learned how to distinguish the essential. To see what is essential in a child, one must have a vagabond look, a look that strolls unhurried over the child who is playing. A child playing is a happiness that passes very quickly. The eyes of parents are administrative eyes. They try to administer infancy, thinking that this can guarantee the future. (Fools, they don't even know if there will be a future...) The eyes of grandparents are wise eyes, wise in the precise sense of the etymology of the word *sapient*. *Sapio* in Latin means "I savor." Children are objects of savoring.

I really feel sorry for children. They are victims of their parents' disturbances. How much wrong is done to them, from sadistic beatings and torture that often end in death, to the normal, daily wrongdoings done with the razor of a look or the punches of the voice. And they, poor little things, children, are weak. There's nothing they can do. The only thing they can do is shrink back in fear. Infantile reason can't do anything against the adult arguments of force. Dostoyevsky tells about one of these victims of parental malfeasance—alone on a cold night, closed in a dark room, as punishment for some transgression she'd done. And she beats on the door with her little hands, crying... And the author comments that nothing, absolutely nothing in the whole universe, can justify or pardon such cruelty.

I really like children's stories, the old ones, the classics, with all their horror. The Disney films ruin them. The horror is taken out. The classics are transformed into cute little stories. Robbed of the horror, they become innocuous diversion. They lose their power of revelation and recovery. The old stories weren't written for enjoyment. They were written to horrify. Often it's in horror that revelations and transformations happen.

In the Old Testament there is a wonderful incident. King David seduced and impregnated Bathsheba, wife of Uriah, one of his generals who was off at war. Not knowing what to do, David imagined that the death of Uriah would get him out of that intolerable situation. He gave orders to his captains to abandon the cuckolded husband during combat so he would be killed by the enemy. That they did. Crime consummated, the prophet Nathan came before the king and told him of a situation, asking the king for a decision.

"A rich man had thousands of sheep that he loved very much. His neighbor was a poor man who had just one sheep, which he loved very much. So the rich man, wishing to eat some mutton, stole the single sheep from his neighbor, killed it and ate it." The king, infuriated with the story, rendered his sentence: "Let that man be killed." The prophet looked the king in the eye and said, "You are that man."

That's how the trap-stories go. You think they're talking about someone else in a distant land many years ago, and all of a sudden you realize that that story is our story. We talk about the story of Snow White, the story of Cinderella, and we think they are false stories that never happened—once upon a time in a land far away—we don't realize that they are happening in our own house.

Reading these stories, I imagine the situations that would have brought them about. I know they were born from wounds. Stories are the bleeding that runs from wounds.

From what wound does the Cinderella story run? The suffering of a child.

Who made it up? I think it was an old nanny who looked at the girl with the eyes of a grandmother. She was the one who made the girl sleep in the maid's bed while the ball took place in the salons on the other side of the closed door. She told this story to make the girl sleep.

The story tells of a stepmother. Women who do what that one did could only be stepmothers. But was it really a stepmother? Storytellers know that real names cannot be spoken—as in dreams. The nanny was afraid to say the real name. It is dangerous to denounce the boss. I don't think it was a stepmother. I think it was the mother herself.

Disney made a sweet interpretation of the story. The stepmother was real, evil, and ugly. Her two daughters were horrible and spiteful. The three could not stand the beauty of the husband's daughter. Gnawed with jealousy and taking advantage of the father's absence, they tried to get her out of the way. They shut her off in the kitchen.

But there's another hypothesis to consider. Mother and three sisters. Of the three sisters, two were pretty and smart. The third was disheveled and ugly—possibly with a deformed foot. If she had had a normal foot, there's no way to explain the fact that only one shoe fit on her foot. Some other girl in the kingdom must have worn the same size. It is even possible that she had Down Syndrome. The girl was a cause of shame, a cause of embarrassing scenes.

When the mother looked at her two pretty daughters, her eyes smiled. And the girls knew it. But when she looked at the other daughter, her eyes filled with shame. And the girl felt it.

She was the mother of the first two. Because a mother can be seen by her look.

The third was aborted by the mother's look. Now, at a time when so much is discussed about abortion, religious people don't notice that among animals, motherhood is a matter of uterus. It's not like that among humans. Human beings are created in the eyes of mothers. The eyes have the power to communicate beauty or ugliness, to transmit life or death.

It is certain that the mother of the first two daughters was the stepmother of the third. The girl caused her shame. How to explain to others (Oh, the eyes of others, the traps of our body!) that the girl was her daughter, that she had come from within her? She could not stand not being able to show that daughter to the eyes of other mothers in the game of comparisons and envy into which mothers and fathers throw their children.

That was the girl who was put in a place "far from eyes," in there with the ashes and cinders. What was her name? It is not known. We only know her nickname: *Cinderella,* she whose body was made of ashes. Or *Cinder Cat*[3], she who was with the cats in the cold, sleeping beside the warm cinders to stay warm. She didn't enjoy the happiness of human warmth in a mother's eyes. That kitchen where she lived was the eyes of her stepmother.

---

[3] In Brazil, Cinderella is known as the *Gata Borralheira*, literally, the "Cinder Bin Cat," i.e., the cat that slept where the warm cinders were.

IV
Andante Con Espressione

with the soundtrack of the film
Like Water to Chocolate

Barbecues

There was a time when I was a vegetarian. Not for a diet or religion. It just happened. I was studying the life of Gandhi with the intent of writing a long poem, *A Magia de Gestos Poéticos*, and all of a sudden, against my will, meat nauseated me. So I became, for reasons of soul, vegetarian. Upon finishing the book, I made peace with the flesh of animals.

At a congress I was questioned about my eating habits. They thought my style of writing and my love of animals demanded that I be vegetarian. They obliged me to confess: "Do you eat meat?" I answered honestly. "If I were king, emperor, dictator, I would hand down a vegetarian decree, for the protection of animals. I would say, 'It is terminally prohibited to kill animals for alimentary purposes. From today on, all must eat only things that the earth produces: fruits, vegetables, greens, cereals, etc.' This is my will."

Then I added an anthropological reflection based on a story told to me by Carlos Rodrigues Brandão, a committed vegetarian who loves scorpions, even when he gets stung. He told me about a certain tribe of Indians, cannibals, who ate their deceased loved ones. Accused of barbarism by the civilized, the Indians argued that "You whites are the barbarians. You don't love your dead. You bury them in deep graves to be eaten by worms. But we love our dead. We wish them to continue living. We wish them to go on near us. But for that, there is only one recourse. They will continue to live and will remain close to us if we eat them. They will remain alive and nearby *in* us." Then I concluded: "I wish the same for animals. I love them. I want them to continue alive and nearby. If I were emperor or dictator, I would issue that law. I am not. They are dead. They are already dead. The only act of love left to me is to eat them, so that they can go on living inside me." I don't know if my justification convinced them. In fact, it provoked many a smile.

I am not vegetarian. But I'm horrified by barbecues. Barbecues give me surreal nightmares. As we know, Descartes said that we are what we think: "I think, therefore I am." I am what I think. The German philosopher Ludwig Feuerback, who greatly influenced Marx, disagreed. He said that "we are what we eat." *Being* has something to do with eating.

This aphorism is open to various interpretations. One of them is of psychoanalytical inspiration. I think (psychoanalysts have nothing to do with this heresy) that the body is a stage whereon many actors live. All of them have the same face, but they all wear different costumes. There's a main actor, who occupies the scene most of the time. Once in a while, however, there's a cue that brings another actor out of hiding from behind a curtain and into the scene. At that, the main actor leaves the scene, and the other steals the show. I become the other—an other that I, too, am.

So I think the aphorism "We are what we eat" can be interpreted this way: Food is a "cue" that makes an actor appear, an actor I become while I eat. The *being* that devours a barbecue isn't the same that eats asparagus soup. So I suggest to my psychoanalyst colleagues that to their interest in dreams they add an interest in the feeding habits of their patients. What you eat reveals what you are.

And who is the actor who shows up to eat barbecue? It's the troglodyte who lives within us, the primitive caveman. Do you doubt it? Just go to a Brazilian barbecue place, a *churrascaria* that offers an all-you-can-eat *rodízio* of meats. Your doubts will be eliminated. Is there any show more grotesque than the attack of waiters with the spits full of filets, loins, rumps, steaks, and sausages? What is offensive isn't the meat. It's the spectacle. I have a sadistic project to someday make a film about a *churrascaria*. What would I film? Just the mouths gobbling meat and chewing it up. A man in love would never again invite his date to such a spectacle. Because the *being*—in the philosophical sense—that shows up at the devouring of a barbecue is everything except a loving, romantic being. Lovers prefer asparagus soup. Of course a politician doesn't invite his co-religionists to have soup. It's always a barbecue, a man thing, a macho thing. The barbecue is the most primitive culinary product. Before that, it was raw meat. It happened by accident. The fire lit in the cave for heat. The troglodytes all around with their raw meat. They get sleepy. They sleep. When they awake, the fire has burned the meat. They get mad but resolve to eat it anyway. They discover that the meat has become tender and delicious. Thus the barbecue was invented. The barbecue was the first culinary technique we know of. It was just a matter of throwing the meat on the coals. It took centuries, maybe millennia, for our ancestors to get the idea of spits. The smell of the burnt fat that dripped on the coals is the olfactory cue that the troglodyte within us can come out of the cave where he's hiding.

But my greater objection to the barbecue is of another order. One of the greatest advances in the history of mankind was the control of fire. In the beginning, man did not have the technique of producing fire. Fire happened naturally, the result of lightning Or the spreading of other fires. It had to be "gathered" with burning sticks or embers, taken to the cave and cared for. If it wasn't cared for, it would die. Someone had to be taking care of it. Men went out to hunt. Women stayed in the cave. It fell to them to take care of the fire. Without fire, there was no light, no heat, no food. So they learned the importance of tending a fire. They were the guardians of fire, semi-sacred beings who kept the gift of the gods alive. And so, through the centuries, this division was established: men came and went while women remained to take care of the fire.

So men became envious of women. The myth of Prometheus shows that men are always wanting to steal fire from whoever has it. From fire comes men's fascination with the kitchen—they want to get in there and cook. I remember, back in Minas Gerais, the women throwing their husbands out on holidays. "A man's place is in the street." Translation: you are a hunter. Your place is far from the fire. Around the fire, I'm in charge.

But then something new developed: the barbecue pit. The barbecue pit is outside the kitchen, far from the domain of women. It's a toy fire, ephemeral, on a holiday. It's outside, in the open air, like the good old days of the cave. At the barbecue pit, without messing up the kitchen, the man can play at being the owner of the fire. And the woman, the real owner of the fire, let's him be. And note, even with fondness, how the man plays at being a troglodyte. It's very macho…

Concerto for Body and Soul

Soups

If God told me to choose the food that I would eat in heaven, for eternity, I wouldn't hesitate for a second. I would choose soup. Shrimp, seasoned beef, salmon à Dalí, the most refined dishes—everything would become intolerable after a few repetitions. But that's not true of soup. I can have soup for all of eternity without tiring of it.

My relationship with soup is more than gastronomic. It's a tender relationship. Soup takes me back to the kitchen of my childhood home, to the wood cookstove, the winter afternoons. Dinner was served at five o'clock. Ah! A hot soup on a cold afternoon is a fireplace lit within the stomach. Little by little the heat spreads through the body. With a few drops of pepper, it turns into sweat, and if you don't use a napkin in time, the drops of sweat on your forehead end up in your soup bowl.

To me, soup is a sacrament of intimacy—a present, physical object that has a happiness that was absent. Hot soup takes me to other places, other times. I make and like cold soups. Cold apple soup, for example, has an exotic flavor. It pleases my palate. But these sophisticated soups lack the sacramental element. They don't take me anywhere. They lack the heat to take me back to an intimate space.

Soup is food for the poor. Fine soup, cream of asparagus, cream of heart of palm, cold apple soup, is posterior nobility. The fundamental soups are made with leftovers. Only the poor save leftovers. Soup is the food of war, of hunger, when any scrap of food is precious and cannot be wasted. The rich don't save leftovers. They don't need to. It's humiliating. The leftovers of the rich go to the trash. The leftovers of the poor go into the soup pot. The fundamental soups are made with leftovers that were destined for the trash. Soup is a magic potion through which that which was lost is saved from perdition and redirected back into the cycle of life and pleasure.

Bachelard's imagination says that matter also imagines. Water imagines rainbows. Seeds imagine flowers and trees. Marble imagines *Kisses* (Rodin) and *Pietàs* (Michelangelo). Rivers imagine clouds (Heládio Brito). Foods also imagine. The barbecue imagines spits, knives, forks, objects masculine, infernal, and phallic. The barbecue needs perforations, cuts, lacerations. The jaws struggle with the meat. The meat resists.

Soup is tame. It isn't meant to be masticated. The spoon is concave, an emptiness. It is feminine. Nothing is perforated. The movement is that of gathering, not hunting. The spoon gathers[4] without violence. I've always had a problem with the etiquette of snobs for taking soup, the dainty sipping of

---

[4] In Portuguese, "colher" can mean either the noun *spoon* or the verb *gather*.

the soup with the *side* of the spoon, not with the beak of it. Now, now, I have argued by analogy that people should eat solid food from the side of the fork—which isn't possible. It's a fact. Not possible. The fork belongs to the ranks of pointed, perforating utensils. They enter head-first. The spoon belongs to the ranks of discreet, modest utensils. They go in sideways, gently.

Salvador Dalí, when he was a boy, dreamed of being a cook. He preferred painting and produced his marvelous surrealist paintings. Realism, in painting, is guilt on the presupposition that things are what they seem to be, nothing more, nothing less. The eyes, facing a realist painting, never experience the surprise of the impossible or the unthought. Realism confirms what all eyes see. Surrealism, to the contrary, believes that that which the eyes see has very little in common with reality. If we look with attention, we perceive that things are at the same time what they seem and something else—elephants reflect in the water of a lake like swans, scenes compose the erotic body of a women, the body of Christ is transparent and through him we see seas, mountains, and boats. Realism confirms the created. Surrealism recreates the created.

Soups are a culinary version of surrealism. If he had gone into his first vocation, Salvador Dalí would have been a soup specialist. For soups are made *negating* things in their brute, natural reality and transforming them by means of unusual relationships that the *broth* makes possible. The broth of the soup is the magical medium that brings together in the pot things which in nature were born apart. I think it would be impossible to catalog all the possible combinations: corn meal, wheat flour, potatoes, garlic, carrots, turnip, onion, tomatoes, peas, eggs, squash, manioc, yams, sweet potatoes, meat, fish, chicken, shellfish, cabbage, collards, beets, asparagus, spices, peppers, oregano, rice, cheese, olives, bread, apples, avocado—a rice soup isn't really rice soup if it doesn't have mint leaves. And we can't forget that soup is the only food that can be made with stone, as in the classic story told to children and adults.

I also like soups because they are entities from the world of wizards, witches, and sorcerers. In the world of magic, there's no barbecue. Wizards, witches and sorcerers make their potions in enormous soup kettles, as was the case of Panoramix, the druid of Asterix and Obelix, who prepared their brew of unbeatable strength in a kettle of boiling soup.

I prefer rustic soups—and making them gives me great pleasure. A cornmeal soup in its many versions, kale soup, rice soup with mint leaves, a multicolored soup of vegetables: soups are always a joy. Rustic soups give us permission to throw in chopped bread. Is there anything happier than that? I get together with some friends on Mondays to read poetry over a dish of soup.

One last bit of information: soups are wonderful medicines for depression. When a hot, aromatic, colorful, peppery soup hits the stomach, sadness leaves and joy returns. No melancholy resists the magic of a bowl of soup.

Concerto for Body and Soul

Rice and Beans, Ground Beef and Tomato

Let me be unpolished and direct. There are occasions when there is no time for courtesy or beating around the bush. It's later than you imagine.

You think your life is stupid, that it's nothing like what you dreamed it would be. You who turn your nose up and refuse to eat the rice and beans with chopped beef and tomato that's set before you, claiming that you deserve caviar and lobster. Let me tell you that it's better to come to your senses and eat the rice and beans with chopped beef and tomato there on your plate. It's delicious, especially with a little hot red pepper and love.

Leave your gripes for when there's a reason for them—when your wife dies of leukemia and you're alone, when your husband is out of work and sinks into depression, when your son dies in a car accident, when the doctor tells you that you have cancer. No, I'm not playing Pollyanna's happy game, nor am I using that old argument, "a lot of people have it worse than you." The happy game is a game of lies. And the game of "a lot of people have it worse than you" doesn't console. The misfortune of the other guy isn't reason for me to be happy. I'm just trying to call your attention to the reason. What I am saying is that you can't blame life for your unhappiness. You have to blame yourself. It isn't life that's ruining you. It you who are ruining life.

I am more and more impressed with people's insanity. What would you tell someone who goes through life spreading feces wherever he goes? They do that and then complain that life stinks. With good reason. The number of people unhappy because of the stink of their own feces is much greater than you think. So be careful when you whine about life. Whines about life often reveal the intestinal disturbances of those who whine.

My advice is that you carefully examine your eyes. You fear people with an evil eye, those whose eyes gush with a malevolent power that kills everything it touches. I've heard reports of ferns that have dried up in a day from the caustic power of the evil eye.

As for the power of other people's evil eyes over our lives, I can say nothing, not even whether I believe it. But I can say that I believe in the power of our evil eye over our own lives. Rice and beans, with chopped beef and tomato, seen with an evil eye, is the food of a beggar.

Jesus, wise knower of the secrets of the body and soul, said that "the eyes are the lamps of the body. When the light of our eyes is black, the world is sunk in darkness. When the light of our eyes is colorful, the world becomes a rainbow." The world doesn't change. The eyes that we see it with change. And the least little thing becomes a reason for amazement. William Blake spoke of "seeing a world in a grain of sand and a sky in a wild flower." But evil eyes see the opposite. Before the radiant world, they only see stone, and beneath a starry sky they only see feces.

It isn't your life that's going badly. It's your soul.

In the waiting rooms of ophthalmologists there are usually those colored pictures, with longitudinal cuts for the eyes, that explain how people see. It happens the same way as with a photographic camera: the light comes from outside, passes through a little hole, crosses a lens, and goes on to the back to leave an image of an object that the light reflected off of.

This holds true for the fact of vision, from the perspective of physics. But that's not how we see. Blake says that "the tree that a fool sees isn't the same tree that the wise man sees." Bernardo Soares explains that this is so because "we only see what we are."

I advise you to take care of your eyes. Take care of them! They have a look of innocence. It seems they are never guilty of anything. The fact is that they are capable of terrible things. It is through them that the garbage that lives within us slips out into the world and plagues it.

Always take with you a bottle of anti-envy eye drops. Envy is an ocular disease still unidentified by ophthalmologists. But everyone has experienced it. It is characterized by disturbance in the movement of the eyes. At least that's how it's described by Fernando Pessoa, who beseeched the gods to free him from "envy, which makes the eyes move." Let me explain. You are before a dish of rice and beans, chopped beef and tomato, a whiff of pepper and love! Pure childhood delight! The body smiles, anticipating pleasure. Then the eyes make a lateral motion. They see that your neighbors are eating caviar with lobster. When your eyes come back to your plate of rice and beans with chopped beef and tomato, they no longer see your happy childhood dish. They see the plate of a beggar, and the joy disappears.

If you don't have the eye drops, read the little book *Duas Dúzias de Coisinhas à-toa que Deixam a*

> *Birds at the window*
> *flannel pajamas*
> *brigadeiro candy in the pan.*
> *A cat walking on the roof,*
> *the smell of wet woods*
> *old record without a hiss.*
> *Warm bread in the morning*
> *mint drops*
> *the call of Tarzan*
> *Drawing a lucky straw*
> *drop pebbles into the well*
> *a scarf around the neck.*
> *Parrot that talks*
> *stepping onto a Persian rug*
> *I love you and vice-versa.*
> *Lightning bug lit in the hand*
> *hot days in the summer*
> *a hand along the bannister.*
> *Sunday supper*
> *flight of flamingos*
> *a hero who smokes a pipe.*
> *Gnome in the garden*
> *satin bow*
> *to finish the book this way:*

Concerto for Body and Soul

From the Zen tradition comes this story I'd like to tell you:

> A man was in a dark forest. All of a sudden he heard a terrible roar. It was a lion. Terrified, he took off running like crazy. He didn't look where he was going. He fell over a cliff. In a panic as he fell, he grabbed a branch. And there he was, between the lion above and the abyss below. Then, looking at the wall of the cliff, he noticed a strawberry plant. And on the plant, a fat, red strawberry. He reached out one arm, picked the strawberry, and ate it. It was delicious.

And that's the end of the story.

It's already later than you imagine. Don't lose the good moments that life is offering you while you hang over the abyss. A moment may arrive when you come to say, "What a shame I didn't eat, with joy, the rice and beans, the chopped beef and tomato." But then it will be too late. Remember: the past has passed. There is nothing to regret. The future has yet to arrive. There is nothing to enjoy. The only thing we have is the moment. Don't lose the now!

In time: The author of *Duas Dúzias de Coisinhas à-toa que Deixam a Gente Feliz*, Otávio Roth, never saw his book published. He couldn't eat his own strawberry. The tree branch from which he hung broke off. He fell into the abyss.

V
Sincopado

by Paul Furlan
Concerto for Gargle, Cash Register, and Honk,
with accompaniment

On Crime and Intelligence

I remember Sherlock Holmes's pipe. I do not remember his gun.

Hercules Poirot's mustache, I remember. His gun I do not remember.

I remember Detective Columbo's rattletrap car. His gun I do not remember.

Famous detectives. They didn't use guns. They worked with their heads. They combatted crime with intelligence.

The book *Journey to Ixtlan* contains the wisdom of an Indian sorcerer, Don Juan. Carlos Castañeda, anthropologist, was curious to know how Indians used hallucinogenic plants. He befriended a little old man, hoping that he could give him some leads on finding the information he wanted. He didn't know that the little old man, D. Juan, was a sorcerer. Castañeda went in search of science. He found wisdom. The book contains the wisdom of D. Juan. One day, walking through the brush, the two talked about the art of hunting. D. Juan told him, "The hunter isn't the one who knows how to set traps. The hunter is the one who knows the habits of the prey." Shotguns and nets do not the hunter make. Shotguns and nets are not capable of getting prey. For that, the hunter needs to know the habits of the prey. Knowing those habits, the hunter waits in the right place. And then the prey is a goner.

That's how Sherlock Holmes, Hercules Poirot, Columbo did it. The looked to discover the habits of their prey. They gathered clues with the certainty that, if put together, the clues would reveal the logic the criminal worked under. Once the clues were put together like pieces of a puzzle, the criminal's face would appear.

Crimes have logic. They don't happen without reason. The criminal always has a motive for his crime. So, faced with the murdered victim, the detective asks a fundamental question: "What would the motive be?" The fundamental hypotheses are summarized in two bits of advice: *Look for the money! Look for the woman!* Or, in a more rigorous philosophical translation, "Crimes happen either for reasons of power or reasons of love."

Life is always full of desires. Little desires, big desires. But, unfortunately, it is not always possible to take possession of the desired object. There is the wonderful tree, full of red fruit. It would be so good if I could eat at least one! But the tree is guarded by a ferocious dog. The dog is the obstacle that stands between my desire and its realization. My desire could be realized if I kill the dog. I commit the crime. I kill so that I can appropriate the desired object for myself.

Crimes are committed in order to eliminate the obstacle that interposes itself between my desire and the object that would satisfy it. Crimes of love: I kill the other so I can possess the object that I love. Crimes of politics: I kill the one who threatens my possession of power. Crime of economics: I kill so that I can possess the item that I desire.

Killing for love, for money, for power: These motives have always existed and always will. Until the end of time, as long as there are unresolved desires and human obstacles to their realization, there will be murder, the murdered, and detectives.

But the world of Sherlock Holmes, Hercules Poirot, and Columbo was another world. The crimes were accidents in an ordered society. A note out of tune in the piano—the detective quickly tunes it anew. From outside, citizens take note of the crimes as curious and emotionally involved spectators who had nothing to do with the plot of the crime. The crimes do not threaten them. Their routines continue imperturbable.

Today things have changed. Crimes no longer happen according to a logic of personal desires. When the murder is carried out in an individual way, the criminal is conscious that his act was a crime, something that violated the laws of society. That's why he hides. He tries to have no one know of his act. Today crimes are of a different order. They are collective acts. Murder, when carried out collectively and independent of individual desires, has the name "war." Carried out collectively, crime takes on virtue because the referential of the criminal is the society of the criminals. Saint Augustus, in *City of God*, talks about the situation when bands of criminals, because of their number and firepower, constitute de facto states without a State, establishing rules for coexistence and their own laws. Unlike the individual criminal, who never thinks about subverting the social order, the collective crime is subversive, an act of political dimensions. It is born from a criminal social order that, according to the standards that society itself sets, isn't criminal. For the criminals, their social order is just and correct, in opposition to the other society, which can be invaded and violated. As it expands as a collective phenomenon, the world of crime establishes itself as a state because its crimes increase along with impunity. Crime, today, follows the logic of war. Sherlock Holmes, Hercules Poirot, and Columbo aren't enough. To combat it, strategists are needed.

For war, as for individual crime, D. Juan's wisdom is true: what is important isn't the weapons; it's intelligence. The French built the most fantastic fortified barrier ever known, the Maginot line—cannons pointed to the east to protect them from the Germans. They did not notice that, by doing so, they revealed their logic to their enemies: the logic of the turtle. At the beginning of the Second World War, the cannons couldn't fire a single shot. The Germans, being intelligent, went around it. The Maginot line was taken over from the rear. The French operated with the logic of the volume of weapons. The Germans operated with the logic of lightness. France was defeated. The generals who commanded the war operations did not need to use machine guns. It was enough to use the brain.

Today, when discussing combating crime, government leaders only argue in the logic of the Maginot line: they talk about the number of police cars (the sound of sirens is worth a motorcade), the power of firearms, the number of soldiers, the visible police patrols. (You recall the times when night watchmen went around blowing whistles all night? I never understood the reason for the whistles. Was it to warn the thieves that they were coming? The whistle blew; the thief hid and waited for the guard to pass. It's the same with overt policing—to tell the crooks that they need to work somewhere else...)

I would really like to have heard the intelligent talk of strategists—those who work with their heads. I would like to know the logic of that war. Organized crime learned from the Vietcong. They adopted the logic of guerrilla war. The political leaders learned from the North American generals. They increased their firepower. The Vietcong won the war, thanks to their intelligence, while brute power was defeated by an excess of weapons and a lack of intelligence. It's sad to imagine that it's possible that criminals are more intelligent and creative than the government.

Concerto for Body and Soul

The Hyena Invasion

What I was little, back in the state of Minas Gerais, after dinner, around five in the afternoon, it was nice to see the fields of hay in the distance, pinkish velvet carpets lit by the sun. In front of the house there was a little pasture where horses that wandered around loose kept the grass low and well trimmed. My father put a wicker chair on the porch, lit up his pipe, and the men of the neighborhood would come over and squat on the grass, sitting back on the heels of their boots. It was a time of endless bullshit. The body and soul were calm. There was no fear. Nothing was likely to happen.

The town square was a continuation of the house, especially for the poor. To be in the street was to be at home. That's what my my father's wicker chair said. I think it was as happy on the sidewalk as in the parlor. And it's still like that in many places — always in poor neighborhoods. I think it was in Fortaleza — a city that surprised me — when I felt something that I had forgotten. It was that cities can be good, civilized places. Walking around a neighborhood of simple people, I was invaded by a sudden childhood happiness. Everybody was in the street. The sidewalks were occupied with chairs, children were playing, grown-ups were talking. They could do that because there was no fear.

That's how the spaces of my childhood were. I had no fear. I walked all over the place as if it were my back yard.

Of course there were crime and criminals. But that didn't make us sneak around with suspicion. The crimes didn't scare people. They didn't threaten us. They were isolated events committed by isolated men. Some were crimes of love. Passion drives men crazy. And there were political crimes. Power drives men crazy. Criminals lived in jail. There were few for so much space. The doors were left open. The prisoners played checkers with the jailers and made wooden wheels that boys bought to make little cars. My little cars didn't have wheels with bearings because the streets of my neighborhood were dirt.

What we were afraid of was the night, not robbers and criminals. Afraid of souls from the other world and ghosts who, back then, appeared frequently. But if my memory is true, there was no record of them doing anything bad to anybody. Our fear was useless. We are also afraid of cat burglars. Cat burglar is a term you don't see very often anymore. I checked the *Aurélio* dictionary, but it didn't clarify anything. I'd like to know if *cat burglar* has anything to do with cats. I think it does. Cats have always existed, and cat burglars, creatures of the night, have existed since ancient times. Cat burglars waited until night fell and people went to sleep. Then they entered their houses. That's how it was long ago. Criminals were afraid and did their work at night, so no one would see them. But the fact was that nocturnal cat burglars were rare.

The authorities took care of safety. And they even had time to take care of stray dogs who walked around the city. They even had a terrible van, which we children hated because we liked the dogs. There were rumors about the sad end that awaited the poor dogs, a rumor that was later confirmed in the film *The Lady and the Tramp*.

The dogs of long ago were humble and humiliated animals. They fled with their tails between their legs whenever people threatened them. Then, all of a sudden, cities were invaded by a new breed of dog with a savage look and threatening teeth. They weren't afraid to attack. Then jackals came. Then hyenas. Town squares and streets were filled with fear. At any moment, at any place, you could be attacked by a wild dog. Cities turned into a place of danger where it was risky to walk.

In the old days, there were few dogs. They were kept in kennels. Today they are uncountable. It isn't possible to catch them. City dwellers have come to a terrible conclusion. If they wanted to be safe, and if it was impossible to keep the dogs in kennels, there was only one solution. They closed themselves inside kennels. And that's how urban transformation came to our cities.

Whoever had a garden in front of the house put up a high wall, bought a guard dog, and installed an electric gate. Today's thieves aren't cat burglars who, in fear and prudence, sneak in at night. They have no fear, nor do they need prudence. They enter the house during the day together with the owners as soon as they open the door to their fortified house. So the owners imagine that they'll be safe if they build greater fortifications—condominiums surrounded by high walls and guards at the entrance. But this is also futile. Guards, too, are mortal and have fear. They can do nothing to stop guns. So the rich think that with private guard dogs, the outside dogs will run away. They hire security guards. But there are more than a few cases of security guards teaming up with criminals. Other people abandon the house with the garden and the dog and move to apartments under the illusion that the wild dogs can't get in. But that's just an illusion. There is no place where they cannot get in. There is no place that can resist their teeth. So some fools say: Let's arm ourselves." As if it were possible to confront the teeth of dogs by using the teeth of tigers. There is no way to escape.

* * *

He and she—young friends. They happily go to the house of a friend for a night of fun. They're just arriving when their car is cut off by another. It's three assailants, guns in hand, one of them a woman. They get into the car and put the two friends in the back seat. They want money. But the friends are students. They have too little money and no credit cards. The robbery is foiled. Frustrated assailants are dangerous. That's why Father Narciso was killed—because he didn't have any money. (In some places people go out with robbery money—not so much that it will hurt if lost, but not so little that the thieves will get mad.) Now the two in the back seat had another problem. The car left the city and went down unknown roads. One of the assailants spun the barrel of his revolver and said, "We need to get rid of these two..."

The young girl was my daughter. They were not killed. They were only abandoned in a remote place. Happy ending. Just luck. Flávio Luiz had no such luck. He was killed. They could have been killed, too. And nothing would happen to the assailants. Nothing would be left to me but sadness and hatred.

I ask myself about the limits of fear. How far can we take it without becoming paralyzed by it or overtaken by irrational anger? Is there no way out? Are we doomed? Inertia and custom makes us stay put. We expect action from the authorities. They don't act. First, because they don't feel like it. They themselves haven't been victims. Second, because they lack the competence. They lack the intelligence necessary to look for solutions. And, finally, because they lack courage and indignation.

So I have noticed that the film *The Lion King*, which I saw for enjoyment with my granddaughters, wasn't enjoyable. It was prophecy. We are at the mercy of hyenas. The film had a happy ending. The Lion King saves the animals. Unfortunately for us, there is no such hope.

Concerto for Body and Soul

Leaf-Cutters and Bandits

I feel sorry for the kids of today. So many things that were fun for me can't be fun for them because these things have simply ceased to exist. Such is the case of the leaf-cutting ants. One sunny afternoon after a rain, thousands of leaf-cutters went flying by in an unforgettable show. Adélia Prado couldn't imagine how God, up in Heaven, would have the beauty of a flight of leaf-cutters, those winged mini-angels. In her poem "A Catecúmena" [The Catechumen] she says:

> *If that which is promised is incorruptible flesh,*
> *that's what I want, he said, and added:*
> *plus the sun on an afternoon with leaf-cutters…*

Ah! My dear Adélia, confusing theologians is your pleasure. I swear, even without having proof, that no theologian has ever written about the leaf-cutters' place in God's plan for salvation. Creatures of divine happiness, creatures of a girl's happiness:

> *Father, digging the ground showed it to us,*
> *with the eye of the hoe, the idiot animal,*
> *the snake with two heads.*
> *He exuded the odor of oil and grease,*
> *workshop sweat, the nasty good aroma.*
> *We had eaten a hot dinner,*
> *pepper and smoke, polenta and mustard.*
> *Stepping on the ground he'd dug up,*
> *he gathered ants flying low,*
> *in the gold dust of five o'clock.*

For kids today, poor things, leaf-cutters are no more than literary figures found in poems.

But leaf-cutters are good for more than poetry. They are also good to eat. Their fat little butts, fried, were delicious. It is said, in passing, that this characteristic of the abdomens of the ant was a naughty metaphor in a song by Juca Chaves: "The beauty of a woman isn't in her face, its in her curse, it's in her cursing..."⁵

But setting aside the poetry, gastronomy, and eroticism of the leaf-cutters, we must not forget that each leaf-cutter carries in its fat belly an entire ant colony of flying ants. This is why elementary schools have contests—whoever catches the most leaf-cutters wins a box of colored pencils. Because it was known in those days that the big problem wasn't in the bad distribution of income or in inflation. It was in leaf-cutter ants. "Either Brazil does away with the leaf-cutters or the leaf-cutters will do away with Brazil"—a motto worthy of appearing on a flag. When the leaf-cutters flew up, the kids came running out, boxes in hand to pick up the ants and take them back to the school. The ants' fate, no one knows. I imagine that they ended up in a fried dish with beer...

---

⁵ This makes more sense in Portuguese. The leaf-cutter ant is a *tanajura*. The sound of the word could also be expressed as *tá na jura,* meaning, "it's in her cursing."

Ants are a terrible plague. They form an absolutely cohesive, authoritarian society without opposition, without political parties or strikes. They are a survival machine with unlimited replacement of losses. It is useless to kill ants wherever they appear. Their appearance is only an incursion of guerrillas. It was by studying ants that guerrillas learned to make war. Against stupid, weighed-down traditional armies, guerrillas pull off quick, unexpected attacks, then disappear. If they hold on to territory, the armies come back with tanks and planes. Like ants. The turf of ants is the anthill, a hideout far from the eyes of the gardener, often in the garden of a neighbor. Ants come up out of cracks, veins, holes, invading the house, advancing on sweets, sugar bowls, attacking food. Attacked by the terrible pismires, we smack them dead. In the house, we wash them down the drain of the sink. We attack armies on the march with insecticides. It's futile. More appear to replace the dead. In the garden we put up fortifications around the trees, but they always find a way to get through.

There's only one way to do away with ants: find their hideout, the anthill. If the anthill is not destroyed, our little retail-level liquidations are useless.

People are curious to know how ideas come to appear in the head of an author. With so many important things to talk about, Rubem stoops to talk about leaf-cutters and other ants. Leaf-cutters and other ants come through poetic inspiration. They pop up as a metaphor of bandits. Long ago, bandits were solitary beings: possums who once in a while get into a house to steal bananas, armadillos that invade gardens to eat the delicious palm bulbs. It was all resolved with a dog or a shot. The crime was a solitary enterprise. It happened at the retail level. The criminals were sidewalk vendors who feared the cops. Today, with this globalization thing, crime has become a corporation of major economic impact. It works in a rational way. They have learned the tactics of ants. They work militarily, like guerrillas: quick, precise incursions, and then they disappear into their anthills.

Imagine a gardener who buys hammers and puts them in the garden. "It's to kill ants when they appear. I am going to kill the ants with a hammer," he explains. There is no ant, in fact, that can resist the blow of a hammer. This is the tactic of police forces—more cruisers, more modern weapons, more police in the streets: hammers waiting for the crooks when they appear. Futile. Guerrillas always attack by surprise. Regular soldiers lose. To protect ourselves, we construct fortresses all around. We end up living in concrete boxes called buildings. We surround ourselves with walls, sentry-boxes, armed guards—condominiums. Two innocent cars arrive. All of a sudden, heavily armed men jump out. Guards and revolvers are worth nothing. The garden has been invaded by ants. The condominium has been taken by bandits.

St. Augustine, describing how States came into being, said this: In the beginning there was a little group of evildoers. Crime here, crime there, constant chases and getaways. In time, the group grew, because stronger, took control of a territory, established a government, turned itself into an army. When this came to pass, he says, the little group of evildoers turned into a State—not because all of a sudden it had become just but because impunity was increasing along with the crimes. Which is precisely our case. There is a State inside of and opposed to the State.

Many years ago, the military concluded that the country was in danger because communist subversives were operating. "A subversive" is whoever plans to destroy the State. They mounted a military operation and did away with the "subversives." But the "subversives" were weak. The only thing they had to offer was an "idea." They wanted a socialist society. Crime today does not work with ideas. It works with money. It's a company. Money has a great power to convince. So the criminal state is much stronger than the state of the subversives. It has a lot more subversive power—the power to seduce the forces of law: that crime can pay more.

I would like it if the police and military forces grant that there is a subversion underway. I would like even more that they learn to exterminate the ants. The anthills need to be destroyed. The police/military forces aren't fools. They know where the anthills are located. So rather than post themselves like hammers in the gardens, I suggest that, after learning guerrilla tactics and how to do away with ants, they post themselves at the anthills. It's the anthills that need to be destroyed. If the anthills are destroyed, the gardens will not need to be protected.

Concerto for Body and Soul

The Fire Is Coming...

The silk floss tree was gigantic.[6] Actually, I don't know if it was really gigantic or if I was small. I know that it was very old. Its bark was dark and wrinkled. Where the trunk went into the earth, there was a big, dark, bottomless hole. In the afternoon, after dinner, the men of the neighborhood sat around on the roots of the tree to roll corn husk cigarettes and tell stories. Many were ghost stories. We kids listened in terror. Once we heard some prophesy about the end of the world. That the world would come to an end was a sure and inevitable thing. Because everything that has a beginning has

---

[6] Ceiba speciosa, a deciduous tree with flowers resembling hibiscus flowers. The trunk is studded with prickles that deter animals.

an end. Everyone agreed that if the first time the world drowned in a flood of water, sparing only Noah and his animals, the second would be by fire. No one would be spared, for we can make no arks to float above fire. And we imagined the terrible scene, the fire falling from the sky like rain, the same way it happened at Sodom and Gomorrah and at Herculaneum and Pompeii.

A Sunday afternoon. The sky was absolute blue, thinned by an excess of sunlight. Suffocating heat coated the face with drops of sweat that ran down. Not a single cloud offered shade. No promise of rain to extinguish the bonfire in the middle of the sky. The car ran down the road through a sad scene. Trees were scarce, lost in the poor fields of wild and stubborn grass. If the heat were to continue, the trees and grass would die. No form of life resists heat for long. I remembered the silk floss tree and the prophesies of the end of the world back in my childhood. I realized that the images of our imagination were wrong. The world would not end with a rain of fire that would burn everything in a raging fire. The fire of the end of the world would be more cruel, like the fire of that afternoon, the fire of a low-heat oven roasting slowly.

In times past, the scene was something else. The countryside was green forests where brooks of cool water ran, full of ferns, bromeliads, orchids, animals and birds of every kind. Where there is forest, there is water. Where there is water, there's life. The forests were cut by businessmen, developers, lovers of profit who were short on vision. A tree standing up isn't worth anything to them. A tree on the ground is worth money. They cut the forests to plant coffee and raise cattle. Now the ground is good for neither pasture nor coffee. In a short time it has turned into desert. What was left was the forests in the mountains. The forests in the mountains were saved not out of love but because they were no good for cattle or coffee. What was left was the forests useless to progress and profit. It is in them that green life found refuge—precarious oases in the middle of a desert of development.

That was in the state of Rio de Janeiro. But wherever you go, you find the tracks of businessmen and developers. Fifty years ago, in the region of the city of Governador Valadares, in Minas Gerais, everything was green, alive with forests, springs, and creeks. Men saw the forests and did not love them. They saw them standing up, beautiful and useless, and they figured out their value lying down, dead and profitable. Today, all that's left is a sad countryside where eucalyptus are planted. As soon as they grow, they're cut down and turned into firewood. The fresh perfume of the forest was replaced by the smell of hot smoke.

The same happened with the pine forests of Paraná state, in the south of Brazil. In their place stretches an endless green carpet—the beautiful plantations of soy that get lost at the horizon. Around here are the plantation of sugar cane. Seen from a plane, they look like immense lawns. But they are deserts. In the fields of soy and sugar cane, there are neither trees nor springs nor animals nor birds.

Now the businessmen and developers turn to what is still left: the Amazonian forest. I visited a region of the Amazon forest that had been devastated by profit. It was like a beach. The only thing missing was the sea. Pure sand. Once the trees are cut, the water evaporates and the forest turns into a desert. It is possible that in some not-too-distant future where there was once the Amazon forest there will be only a continuation of the Sahara desert.

A president of the United States once wrote to Indian chief Seattle with a proposal to buy his land. The Indian chief's answer is one of the most beautiful and moving manifestations of love of nature ever produced. He knew what the fate of his land would be if civilization took ownership of them.

> *There is no calm place in the cities of the white man. No place to listen to the blooming of flowers in the spring or the beat of an insect's wings. And what is left of life if a man cannot hear the solitary cry of a bird or the croaking of frogs around a lake*

at night? The Indian prefers the smooth murmur of the wind wrinkling the face of the lake and the smell of the wind in rain or the perfume of pine.

I am horrified by our powerlessness before the destructive power of companies that raze nature for the love of money. But I'm even more horrified to feel that other people are not horrified. They don't love nature. For them, it is natural to treat nature like a garbage dump. I remember the sadness I felt in Pocinhos do Rio Verde. Ahead of me was a pick-up truck of happy, middle-class youngsters who had just graduated from school. They were calmly tossing empty beer cans to the side of the road as if this were the most natural thing in the world. School had taught them many things, but not the essential. Once I took a hike in the Ecological Park and never went back. The sight of soda cans and plastic bottles along the trails just made me mad. They told me that once the entrance exams were over at the PUCC university, a company passed out boxes of soda to the kids as they left. That night the street was piled with trash. At the Unicamp state university at Campinas, São Paulo, there was a day denominated Open University. The day after was tragic. The campus was an absolute garbage dump, covered with plastic bags, cups, bottles, soda cans, paper, napkins and detritus of all kinds. My dear friend Herógenes, a professor and director of the garden, now deceased, told me that after that day all the young trees had to be replanted because the future university students had broken them for pure pleasure.

I believe that the preservation of nature is the most important challenge of the present time. It has to do with the preservation of life, the future of our earth, the future of our grandchildren. It's more important than all the doctrines preached in churches. Because, to believe the sacred scripts, our primordial vocation is that of gardeners. God gave us a mission to take care of Paradise. It's more important than all the science that can be taught in schools. Because all of science will be empty and useless if our work is turned into a desert.

Rubem Alves

I'd like to be able to go back to the silk floss tree in whose shade I first heard the forebodings of the end of the world—just to read a counterfeit sacred script, a prophesy of a new world being born:

> *The poor and needy seek water, but there is none, their tongues fail for thirst.*
> *But rivers shall open in desolate heights, and fountains in the midst of the valleys;*
> *the wilderness shall be made a pool of water, and the dry land springs of water.*
> *In the desert will grow the cedar and the acacia tree, the myrtle and the olive, the cypress and the pine, the elm and the box tree together…(Isaiah 41:17-19)*

VI
Adagio Lamentoso

in contrition
with *Deep Water*
(African-American Spiritual)

Leandro

I looked at his photo, his hands crossed on his chest in a gesture of holding on to life what was preparing to leave.[7] But you didn't want to leave. It wasn't time. You wanted to stay. Life can be quite good. Your sad eyes made me remember verses by Cecília. "Everything in me was an absence that stayed around, a good-bye ready to fulfill itself...And you took on little wings..." His photo told me that his body had already sailed toward "the third bank of the river." And I was moved.

There are people who depart, desiring to leave because the body is tired and the time has come. Tiredness is the time to go. The leave-taking is sad,

---

[7] Luís José da Costa, popularly known as Leandro, was a singer and composer of *sertanejo*, a Brazilian country music that in many areas is more popular than samba.

but it's what must be. Life is made of good-byes. For these good-byes, the tears are sweet. They run like water that blossoms from a gentle spring.

But there are those who leave out of obligation. They leave while wishing to stay. For these, the tears are bitter. They turn into a revolting sea.

You didn't wish to leave. No one wished you to leave.

You know, Leandro: *sertaneja*—Brazilian country music—was never big with me. But, seeing the people who cry at your passing, I feel sorry for myself. If people are crying, it's because the music you sang was bread for their souls. So I know that if I want to understand the soul of the people—if it's possible to understand the soul—I will have to learn to love your music.

Where was God when your body was attacked by the mortal enemy? Why didn't he do anything despite all the appeals? Why did he remain indifferent while you struggled? These are the terrible questions asked by all who believe in God in the face of your absurd death. The death of an old man who lived a long life is not absurd. Death is the natural end of a temporal process, like the end of a song. But there are deaths that are absurd. The death of a small child, the youngster, the mature man and woman full of life. Your death. It wasn't time. Night fell at noon. All absurd. Where was God?

I'm going to talk about God. I must be careful with my words. The wise one of the Old Testament advised: "Do not be rash with your mouth, and let not your heart utter anything hastily before God. For God is in heaven, and you on Earth; therefore, let your words be few." (Ecclesiastes 5:2) God is a word that should not be spoken. Jews were prohibited from pronouncing the sacred name, under penalty of death. Caeiro goes further still: don't even think about it:

> *To think about God is to disobey God,*
> *because God wants us not to know him,*
> *which is why he doesn't show himself to us.*

Words are cages. The spoken is that which reason has caged. A God who can be caged by words is not a God. God is an "Enchanted Bird." For him there are no words.

But men insist on caging God. When they speak of God, they break down. And they show the imprisoned bird. They say, "This is the Enchanted Bird in my cage of words!" They don't notice that it is not a living bird. It's a stuffed bird.

Philosophers and theologians like to talk about God. It's very true that there are exceptions, philosophers who refuse to talk about God, not for disbelief but out of respect. They are content to watch the flight of the Enchanted Bird in silence. Such is the case of the pious Kant and the mystic Wittgenstein. These are philosophers of "modest reason."

Others, possessed by "arrogant reason," set themselves to talking. Saint Anselm (1033-1109) even came to define God as "that of which nothing greater can be conceived" (*Aliquid quo nihil maius cogitari possit.*) God is total knowledge, omniscience. God knows all things, what is, what will be. God is total presence. God is present in all places. The eye of God sees you. God is total power, omnipotence. Nothing that happens happens against his will, from the Big Bang to the beating of the wings of a fly. God, for the man of reason, had to be the consummation of all possible perfections.

If God is thus, if everything is done by his will, then he must be happy. For happiness is exactly in this: the coinciding of that which is desired and that which is. God's supreme perfection is in this: that he is supremely happy. An unhappy God would be an imperfect God, a God without enough power to carry out his will.

Little children die of hunger. Elderly people die in wars. Youngsters die in disasters. Adults die in droughts. Forests die by fire. You, Leandro, died of cancer. God is omnipotent. If he had so desired, you would have lived. But no. The God that the theologian painted is the agent of your disease and of your death. If it happened, it's because he wanted it. If he wanted it, fine. He's happy. And the people confirm it: "God knows what he wants." "It's the will of God." These are the words from the mouths of religious people to explain tragedies. God wants our suffering. Our suffering brings him happiness.

The argument of the logic is perfect. I do not find logical flaws in it. But the logic of the heart is something else. You, Leandro, in the flower of life, died an absurd death. I cannot love a God who became happy with your death, nor even with the death of a simple songbird. A God who does that and has such feelings cannot be the object of anyone's love. Whoever says he loves this God is lying. This god can be the object of fear but not of love. I, a simple mortal, full of imperfections, if I had the power that theologians and philosophers claim is attributable to God, I would not let such things happen. Because I love. Love, when possible, impedes pain. If love does not impede pain, it's because it's weak. It has no power. The love of all those around you, Leandro, was a weak love, powerless before death. That's why they cried. Crying always comes from weak love. That's how people are.

Biblical poems say that God created us in his image. We look like God. When I feel the beauty of nature, I know that God, too, feels it. God feels through my body. When I feel the good taste of a fruit, I know that God is feeling the good taste of it, too. God needs us to feel. When I find that the music you sing is beautiful, Leandro, God, too, finds it beautiful. When my love struggles against suffering and death, God struggles, too. And when I cry over suffering and death—events despite my weak love—God cries, too. His love is infinite. But, contrary to what theological logic says, his power is not infinite. In this he is my equal. This is the drama of the universe: love looking for power to bring happiness back.

The Greeks of mythic times said that the universe is a struggle between Love and Chaos. From Love were born beauty, harmony, order, life, and joy. From Chaos were born disorder, accidents, diseases, pain, the absurd, sadness. God is Love. Love is my God. He lives in the heart of my universe, like a fetus in the belly of a mother. But not yet born. He isn't omnipotent. He fights against Chaos. And he cries over his own impotence. Not even God escapes the blows of Chaos. The "Crucified God" of painter Grünenwald is a model expression of that tragedy. Love wanted you to live, Leandro. But Chaos was stronger. God, too, is crying...

Magnolias and Jabuticabas

I beg your pardon, my readers, for having many deaths to cry over. I would like to put to practice Camus's literary program: "My writings will come from my times of happiness, even the cruel ones." This hasn't been possible for me. I've had many deaths to cry over. So my words drip from my wounds like blood.

It has happened again. A friend of more than thirty-five years became enchanted: Antônio Quinan. Months ago, worried about his heart, he looked for a cardiologist. The results of the exam: his heart was perfect. He calmed down. He didn't know that it wasn't his heart that Death was touching. It was touching another place. It happened at a moment of happiness, when he was doing what he most liked to do—talk about "problems" in Minas Gerais with friends at a party. Death hit him while he was smiling.

I went to say good-bye at the wake in Belo Horizonte [capital of Minas Gerais].

Wake. Awake. I refused to sleep. My eyes studied his dead body. Not so long ago he was laughing, unsuspecting of the blow awaiting him. *There are blows in life, so powerful...I don't know! Blows like God's hatred...*The blow...it was he who got hit. But now his impassive face tells us that he no longer remembers it. He suffers no more. We are the ones who suffer, we who remain awake. Uselessly.

A cadaver is a dead body in a circle of silence. The sound of cars in the street, the exhortations of demonstrations, the songs on the radio, the latest tragedies on TV, the daily gripes—it all ceases. The only thing remaining is the confusing noise in a back room, meaningless, a breaking of the silence to which no attention whatsoever is paid. A wake should be in a place where only friends have permission to enter. Because only friends know how to stay silent.

A cadaver is a candle that burns in the darkness. "...Like a votive in a cathedral in ruins..." The candle is awake. A wake. Its flickering light creates a luminescent hemisphere. Inside it a few objects, the essentials, are timidly illuminated by the delicate flame. Everything outside of the glow disappears in the dark.

I remember a verse by Cesar Vallejo...*your cadaver was full of the world.* Cadavers full of worlds?

Padre Antônio Vieira[8] says yes:

> *The speeches of those who have not seen are speeches. The speeches of those who have seen are prophesies. The Ancients, when they wanted to see the future, sacrificed animals, consulted the entrails, and they prognosticated in accordance with what they saw. They did not consult the head, which is the seat of understanding, but the entrails, the place of love. Because the one who understands*

---

[8] Padre Vieira was a 17th century Brazilian Jesuit renowned for his sermons and writings.

> better does not prognosticate better. It's the one who loves. And this custom was throughout Europe before the coming of Christ, and among the other peoples, the Portuguese were unique in this. The others consulted the entrails of animals. The Portuguese consulted the entrails of people. The superstition was false but the allegory is very true. There is no light of prophesy more certain in the world than to consult the entrails of people. If you want to prophesy the future, consult the entrails of people...

Worlds live in the entrails of people. A wake is a magical ritual in which the entrails of the dead are consulted. For this there is no need to open the body. During an entire lifetime, bodies let us see their entrails by means of the mouth. Our entrails aren't viscera, they are words.

Our anxiety over last words! You can believe that my means of last words, the one who is to die voluntarily offers his or her entrails for the contemplation of those who continue to live. (But there is always the danger of not having anything to say. Camus relates the case of a man who, preparing to speak his last words, discovers that he has forgotten them.)

Our last words are a declaration of love. The poet Robert Frost asked that his tomb be engraved with this simple sentence, a summary of his life: "He had a love affair with the world." I think Quinan, if he'd had time, would have said something like that. He loved nature and people with gentleness and tenderness.

I look carefully at the scenery that lived in your body. I see trees growing from your flesh. Gardens. The soul is a garden. Long avenues of magnolias, trees of modest flowers the color of squash. The magnolias can't compete with the beauty of the flowering *ipé*. *Ipés* are gifts to the eyes. They are valued for their color. The magnolias, on the other hand, are gifts to the nose. They are valued for their perfume. The avenue is full of silence and the aroma of magnolias.

I also see a forest of *jabuticaba* trees, the most iconic fruit of Minas Gerais.[9] Bees by the thousands buzz within their white flowers, attracted by the smell. Soon those flowers will turn into fat, round, black fruits (really *fruit*; everybody knows, in Minas Gerais, when the vendor announces *fruit*, it's *jabuticaba* he's selling), clinging to its branches, gleaming after a rain. Sucking *jabuticabas* is a party, a great big game. *Jabuticabas* are kid fruits…

These trees that grow in Quinan's entrails were at the Instituto Gammon, the school in Lavras, Minas Gerais, a place where he grew up, lived, taught, directed, and loved. And died. For it was there, in the celebration of the school's anniversary, that Death hit him.

The magnolias are still there. The *jabuticaba* trees were cut by the orders of a crazy rector under the allegation that street urchins stole the fruits during the night. He, in his idiocy, didn't know that

---

[9] A tree that bears *jabuticaba* fruits sprouting from its trunk and branches. The grape-sized fruits are delicious and somewhat rare because they grow in only a few areas in Brazil and do not transport well.

jabuticabas were created by God with this exact purpose—to be stolen by kids during the night...

For a long time I've had a dream: to make a cemetery. More precisely: to plant a cemetery. Because in it I would not bury cadavers. Rather, I'd plant trees that grow on the bodies of the dead. That way, as beloved people died, I will plant the trees that seem like them. For Betinho, a yellow *ipê*—beautiful even when dry. For Elias Abrão, a sandalwood, a tree my father brought from Lebanon. I'm going to start planting up in the mountains near Pocinhos do Rio Verde, inside the volcano, beside the persimmon trees, near the creek. For Quinan I will plant a *jabuticaba* and a magnolia. When the magnolia blossoms, I will suspect that he's around. When the *jabuticaba* turns black with fruit, I will know that he is around. And so we, with a group of friends, will continue our "affairs" and the laughs that death interrupted...

Concerto for Body and Soul

"A Blue Sky Immensely Nearby…"

I believe, João Pedro, I will never again hear your voice. It was so weak, it was almost a sigh. It seemed to come from another world. And I asked your forgiveness for not having known what to say. We are raised to never have to say the essential words—the last words, words which can only be said in the face of death. Yesterday I called you again. But your wife told me that you had already sunk into the unconscious.

I've always envied you a bit. You were younger and had a trace of arrogance in your profile. I imagined that life had been generous to you. That's when I received one single letter from you. No one had ever written to talk about that subject, one's own death.

I often think about death in general. When I do so, I'm a poet and a theologian. Death is the permanent horizon of theology and poetry. Poetry and theology are a witch's incantation uttered to exorcize death, so that death becomes beautiful and we can die without fear.

I have also written many times about the death of people I love. Faced with the death of friends, the witch remains silent. I am only a friend. And, as a friend, what I know how to do is come up with words for the pain I feel.

But that—writing about my own death—that I have not yet done. Out of pure stupidity. Healthy people are stupid. They do not believe. They live under the illusion of not being mortally ill. They think it's still far off. They need stronger signs, with a date set and a countdown.

You wrote to me, revealing to me that your dialogues with death have begun. It had already sent its messengers and timetable.

Concerto for Body and Soul

Now the countdown is coming to an end. Hearing your voice so weak, I wanted to take it into my lap, as if it were a small child, my child. Everyone who is dying turns into a small child. I had words of neither consolation nor hope to give you. I would like to have been courageous enough to say that, when you died, I cried, that the world became more sad and that I was going to plant a tree inside the crater of the volcano in Pocinhos, beside Elias Abrão's tree, Quinan's tree, mine, and the trees of other dear friends. I would have asked which tree you loved most. But your voice was so weak... And I did not have the courage. I only told you that I loved you and that even from afar I embraced you. From there I saw myself kissing your face—something that I told you, with the crazy rationalization that even men can kiss. If I had remembered, I would have repeated Alberto Caeiro's prayer to the Baby Jesus:

When I die, my young son,
let me be a child, the smallest one.
Take me into your arms and into your house.

Rubem Alves

Take off my tired and human being
and lay me in your bed.
And if I awake, tell me stories,
to put me back to sleep.
And give me your dreams so I can play
until some day I'm born,
some day that you know.

I think coincidences are strange. They say that they don't exist. They are coincidences only for those who don't see the other side of reality. Behind reality, everything is linked, everything has a connection. Arthur Koestler wrote a book titled *The Roots of Coincidence*. Jung, too, wrote on the topic in the introduction to the *I-Ching*. Coincidence or not, the fact is that on Monday, our poetry group day, I went to read Mário Quintana—and all the poems on that day spoke of death.

Earth! Someday you will eat my eyes…
They were
in the meantime
the unique green of your leaves
the most pure crystal of your springs…
My eyes were your painters!

But, in the end, who needs eyes to dream?
We dream with eyes closed.
Wherever you are…where your are…
In the densest dark I will dream of you,
my Earth in bloom!

I soon thought that this would be a wonderful poem to come last in our readings. Last words: What else would be left to be said? I remembered the epitaph Robert Frost chose for his tomb: "He had a love affair with the world." And that's how it was. Mário Quintana's poem is a complaint: "Earth! Someday you will eat my eyes"—eyes that had loved the Earth so much, had painted its leaves and springs. But it didn't matter. Even without eyes, in the densest dark, he went on dreaming of it, "my Earth in bloom!" I imagined that you would smile with approval if I read it in the liturgy of your enchantment.

I went on to this poem:

How hard it is, how hard, Beatriz, to write a letter.
Look! The best thing is to simply describe to you the scenery;
to describe with no images, not one…

each thing is proper for its own wonderful image!
Just now it has stopped raining. No one goes by.
Only a cat crossing the street
as in time almost immemorial
of the silent films...
Do you know, Beatriz? I am going to die!

It's good he tried to hide the thing behind the rain that stopped, the empty street, the cat crossing the street—but it didn't help. The cat slipped out of the description and into a world that no longer exists, and that's how the thing showed up without nexus, purpose, or rhyme. "Beatriz, I am going to die!"

And from there I went on to the last poem, which says everything that I feel:

This sickroom, so deserted
of all, not even books I'm reading
and life itself I left in the middle
like a novel left open.
What difference does this room make, where I
awaken as if awakening in some other room?
I look at the sky! Immensely nearby, yes,
so near and such a friend that it seems

a big blue gaze set upon me.
Death must be like this:
a sky that little by little goes to dusk
and we didn't even know it was the end...

Upon reading these poems—coincidence?—I had the impression that they were being whispered by the gods. And I read them while thinking about you, dear friend, asking the gods not for a miracle (death is stronger than the gods) but that it was for you—for me—as the poet wished:

a blue sky immensely nearby,
a sky that little by little goes to dusk
and we didn't even know it was the end...

Until one of these days, in an encounter in the shade of the trees up in the mountains of Minas Gerais, beside the waterfall, inside the dormant volcano.

Rubem Alves

To Guido, with Affection

He's sad. His wife died. He decides to go to a bar to sit alone in his solitude with a glass of whiskey. He doesn't know where to go. He picks a bar at random. The bar is full. The faces are unknown. None of them interest him. But, all of a sudden, among the unknown faces, he sees the face of a woman. She's alone at a table. "Yes, that's her. She's older, her hair gray, but she's the same..." His face lights up with surprise. So many years they haven't seen each other, since they were young, an interrupted love. She has a lost look. Her arms are on the table, her hands holding a glass. She also came there to endure her sadness. She has just separated from her partner. He comes over. Their eyes meet. They smile. "What a coincidence to find you here!" he says. She answers, "What a coincidence!" And just at that moment, an old song that they used to like to sing together starts to play, like in old times...

Yes, what a coincidence! So many possible bars, so many possible days and times, so many possible songs, but, with no preparation or intentions whatsoever, the things "coincided" to give rise to a happy event. *Co*, which means "together" plus *incidere*, which means "fall on." Coincidence is when two things that have nothing to do with each other happen together, at the same place, like two meteors that, coming from infinite space, hit the same spot at the same time.

Life is full of coincidences like that—suddenly, for no reason, we remember a friend we haven't seen in a long time. The telephone rings, and it's him on the other end. Or there's some question tormenting you, and without thinking or intending anything, you open any old book off the shelf, and there's the answer you were looking for.

Rubem Alves

The word "coincidence" carries the idea that the happy encounter happened by accident...a stroke of luck, like that of someone winning the lottery. But there are many people who don't believe it is an accident. They say that the so-called coincidences, these sudden, meaningful apparitions, are only "apparently" coincidences. Coincidences, according to them, are only manifestations of the invisible web of meaning that connects everything in the universe. Arthur Koestler even wrote a book with the curious title *The Roots of Coincidence*. What the title is saying is that coincidences aren't coincidences, for there are reasons behind them. And Jung wrote in the preface to the *I-Ching*, suggesting that the sticks or coins, tossed apparently in a movement without meaning, manifest reasons that are configured in hexagrams. It's only because of that that the *I-Ching* has its revelatory power.

And, suddenly, Guido shows up at the state university in Campinas to take on the role of attorney general. I don't remember how our friendship got started. I know we became friends. Such good friends that for him, I made an exception. As everyone knows, in an earlier life I was a pastor. I did burials, baptisms, and weddings. But that life ended and I left those things behind. But that didn't help. Like Cain, I take with me a mark on the forehead. In one of the innumerable sessions of regression back to lives unlived to which I submitted myself each day, it was revealed to me that I was the master of liturgy in an extinct monastic order. It just so happens I love liturgy. I baptized my granddaughter Mariana. I've celebrated liturgies with Dominican monks and *mães de santo*[10]. I performed liturgies for weddings. And I have ideas for funerals. Aware of this, Guido asked me to celebrate his marriage to Lenir—a beautiful love story that could have been made a TV novella. I performed the wedding of Guido and Lenir, at the correct astrological time, under the inspiration of the stories *The Girl and the Enchanted Bird* and *The Strawberries*. It was a night of happiness!

---

[10] Literally, "saint mothers," they performed priestly roles in the Afro-Brazilian religion *candomblé*.

I retired. Guido retired. We no longer saw each other at the university. We went on to meet in the "Canoeiros" group, which read poetry on Mondays at my house, after having soup and wine. Or in the Dalí, drinking a whiskey, eating shrimp and listening to *chorinho* music.[11] (Guido is crazy about shrimp fried with garlic, whiskey, and *chorinho*).

It was at one of these meetings that we began to talk about our past. I told Guido that I had passed my adolescence in Rio de Janeiro. He said, "Me, too."

Nothing surprising. Banal coincidence. But I wanted to know details. I asked him what *bairro* he had lived in. Rio is very big, with many *bairros*. "I lived in Botafogo." Botafogo? So did I. Now it's a bigger coincidence. So many *bairros*, and we, friends of the same age, had lived in the same *bairro*. Who knows if we had passed each other. I couldn't resist my curiosity. The street. Which one. Out of so many, hundreds. "I lived on Passagem Street..." he said.

---

[11] *Chorinho* is popular Brazilian instrumental music played with flute, guitar, and ukulele, percussion, perhaps a clarinet or saxophone and other instruments.

My God! Passagem Street! That's where I lived! "Where, Guido? What number?" "I lived at number 36..."

And a smack of absurd coincidence, unthinkable, even in fiction, more impossible than winning the lottery. I said, "I lived at number 35..."

I no longer believe in coincidences. Coincidence with reasons. It seems that the reason behind this absurd coincidence is that we, Guido and I, are in some mysterious way, brothers.

In front of my house there is a garden surrounded by walls. It can be entered through two narrow doors painted blue. In the garden are bromeliads, jasmine, bamboo, vines, and other plants that Paulinho, of "Floríssima" had planted. And a fountain with goldfish. So I had two plaques made. One of them says, "Passagem Street." It will be on the blue door through which Guido transits from the poetry group to the Dalí. On another is written, "Guido Ivan de Carvalho Fountain," which will be affixed over the fountain.

Rubem Alves

Arrival and Departure

In Minas Gerais, in thanks for alms given them by a pregnant woman, beggars bless her with "May Our Lady of the Good Birth be easy on you!" It's a comforting blessing because the time of a pregnancy is a time of pain and anguish, requiring the protection of the Virgin Midwife. When they see it, no one can believe that a baby could pass through such a tight channel. Pain for the mother, anguish for the baby.

In the place where words are born, these shine with shocking brightness. Let me go to the birthplace of the word *anguish*. It comes from the Latin verb *angere*, which means to tighten, to suffocate. So in its birthplace, *anguish* means to say *narrowing*. The baby, who was in a nice place, is going to be tightened and suffocated inside a channel. She's going to feel anguish. And for the rest of her life, whenever she has to pass through a tight, dark channel, she's going to again feel the same thing she felt when she was born. With anguish and pain thus combined, we must admire beggars for invoking the Virgin...

Medicine, an unbeliever in Virgins and beggar blessings, hasn't managed to free the pregnant from anguish and pains. It has tried to; find someone to do the work of the Virgin and care for the women when their time comes. They created a joyous specialty, the oldest of them all, obstetrics. *Obstetrix*, in Latin, means midwife. A literal translation of *obstetrix* is "one who stands before." The midwife is before—in front of—the mother. Before the mother, she watches over the baby. Her function is to help life cross the narrow and agonizing passage from the darkness of the mother's belly to the light of the outside world. [One Portuguese term for giving birth is *dar à luz*.] "To bring to the light." What terrible fantasies must pass through the child when feeling squeezed, dislocated, pulled, yanked, tightened! It's possible the baby feels like he or she is going to die. But, at the end of the strait, the "obstetrix" takes the child up as if she were the mother... She, the midwife, is the first experience of the world that the little child has, the blessed Virgin.

Life begins with an arrival. It ends with a departure. The arrival is part of life. The departure is part of life. Like the day that begins with dawn and ends with a setting sun. Dawn is happy—lights and colors arriving. The setting sun is sad, a final orgasm of lights and colors leaving. Dawn and dusk, joy and sadness, arrival and departure. It's all part of life. It all has to be cared for. People prepare, with care and joy, for the arrival of people they love. It is also necessary to prepare, with care and sadness, for the departure of someone we love.

The orientals know this best. They know that opposites are not enemies. They are brothers. Night and day, silence and music, rest and movement, laughter and weeping, hot and cold, sun and rain, hugs and separations, arrivals and departures. They are the pulsing opposites that give life to life. Life and Death are not enemies. They are brothers. Arrival and departure... Without the words that complete them, the song would not exist. Without Death, life would not exist since life is, precisely, an ongoing departure...

Medicine created obstetrics as a specialty with the mission of "being before" life as it arrives. I think medicine, out of love of mankind, should also create a specialty symmetric to obstetrics with the mission of "being before" those who are dying. Death is also full of fear and pain. Death is also a dark and anguishing strait. It is loneliness. The newborn in the tight, dark canal, is totally alone and abandoned. One who is dying is also absolutely alone and abandoned. Those who love and surround the dying are far away, very far away. The hands they extend do not reach across the abyss. Death is always a sinking into abandonment.

I've thought about this specialty... Isn't the mission of medicine to care for life. The departure is also part of life. Those who are parting are still living... They need as much care as those being born. I even invented a name for the specialty. I combined two words. *Moriens, entis*, from the Latin, which means "who is dying.," and *therapeuein*, from the Greek for "caring for, serving, curing." It came out as *morientherapy*. the caring for those who are dying. And the *morientherapist* would be the one who, similar to the obstetrician, is "before" one who is departing. Our Lady of the Good Birth is the patron saint of women in labor. I looked for another Our Lady to be the patron saint of people who are dying. I found in the *Pietà*, the woman who takes into her lap the son who is dying. To die in the arms of the *Pietà* is, perhaps, to feel yourself finally returning to the lap of the mother you never had but always wished to have. In the lap of the *Pietà*, the departure can be lived, perhaps, as a return to the maternal lap.

Some have told me that this specialty already exists. *Intensivists* are "those who are before" those who are dying. Those who said this did not understand me. The mission of the intensivists is the opposite of what I am saying. Their mission is to impede the departure—at any cost. That's why they are agitated people. At any moment there could be a cardiac arrest—and if they don't run and aren't competent, the departure will take place. Each departure is a defeat. The *morientherapist*, to the contrary, comes onto the scene when hope has been lost. The departure is certain. He or she must be at peace with life and death, must know that death is part of life. It must be cared for. Therefore the morientherapist will have to be a calm being at peace with the end, the end of those in her care, at peace with her own end, when others will care for her. From her no miracles are expected, no heroic recourses to oblige the weak heart to beat for another day. From her all that is expected is care of the body. The departure must be gentle and without pain. And the care of the soul—she must not be afraid to talk about death.

Rubem Alves

I know this will leave doctors embarrassed. They have learned that their mission is to struggle against Death. Once their resources are expended, they leave the arena, defeated and powerless. It's too bad. If they knew that their mission is the care for life, and that death as much as birth is part of life, they would stay until the end. And thus they would become a little wiser. And they would even, I imagine, begin to write poetry...

A Unique Moment

There is a happy death. It's the one that happens at the right time. The king, overflowing with happiness over the birth of his first grandson, invited all the poets, gurus, and wizards of the kingdom to the palace to write in a golden book their good wishes for the child. One wiseman from afar, unknown, wrote: "May your grandfather die, your father die, the son die…" The king, infuriated, sent to have him thrown into the dungeon. The path to the dungeon passed by the king, who cursed him for the words he'd written. The wiseman responded, "Majesty, what is the greatest sadness of a grandfather? Might it perhaps be to see his son and grandson die? What is the greatest sadness of a father Might it perhaps be to see the death of a son? Oh! What wouldn't they give to be able to trade places with the dead sons and grandsons? Happiness is to die in the right order. First the grandfather dies, seeing his sons and grandsons. Then the father dies, seeing his sons..."

Hearing this, the king took the hands of the wiseman in his and kissed them...

I don't believe there is any pain greater than the death of one's child. In the beginning, it is a crude pain, without color or form, like a mountain of stone set on the chest forever. With the passage of time, this crude pain transforms. It becomes many, each one with a different face saying different things. There's that pain that is pure sadness due to absence. It only cries and says, "Nevermore..." Another is that pain of remembering things that were done and should not have been done, things that were not done and should have been done, the word that should not have been spoken, the actions that should not have been taken. It's the pain of longing mixed with the sadness of guilt. And there's another kind of pain: the sadness that the child has not completed what was started.

There is great joy in completing a work that was begun: to see the house ready, the book written, the garden blooming. The life of a child is like that: a dream to be realized. Then comes the impossible meteor that shatters the dream. The house remains unfinished, the book yet to write, the interrupted garden.

This was one of the pains of that father who told me of his pain over the death of his son. I remembered a book I'd read a long time ago, *Lições de Abismo* (Abysm Lesson), by Gustavo Corção. It was the story of a man, fifty-something years old, who found out that he had no more than six months to live. An illness in his body was quickly killing him. With no future, he examines his past, looking for signs that he has not lived in vain. What he finds: shards, fragments, a marriage that fell apart, loneliness. So he thinks that life should have been like a Mozart sonata that lasts no more than twenty minutes. It dies in a short time. Then comes silence. A happy death. The silence is because everything that was to be said has been said. But his life—the record would be broken before he could say anything. His sonata hadn't even begun...

That's how that father felt: his son was a sonata that had barely begun.

If I die now, I won't have anything to complain about. Life has been very generous with me. I've planted a lot of trees. I've had three kids. I've written books. I have friends. Of course I'll feel very sad because life is beautiful despite all its struggles and disappointments. I want to live more. I want to finish my sonata. But if by any chance it remains unfinished, others can take care of finishing it. That's how it happened with Bach's Art of the Fugue. The theme was the notes of his own name, B-A-C-H, B flat, A, C, B natural.[12] On the last page of the manuscript, in the handwriting of Carl Philip Emanuel, son of Bach, is written: "N.B. In the course of this fugue, at the point where the name B.A.C.H. was

---

[12] In Bach's time, and in Germany even today, the b-natural is indicated by the letter h.

introduced as counterpoint, the composer died." Bach died but his work had already been clearly structured. Another ending was possible. If the same happens to me, I won't have anything to complain about. But the question remains. And those who didn't have enough time to write their name?

I've asked myself that question several times, thinking about my kids. I, too, wanted to see them take their sonatas to the end, even if I weren't here to hear them. But that certainly can't be done. The terrible possibility can always happen. And if it happens, the terrible feeling comes that it was all useless.

So, all of a sudden, I experienced *satori*. My eyes opened, and I saw as I had never seen. I felt that time is only a thread. Into this thread are woven all the experiences of beauty and love we've passed through. "That which the memory loved remains eternal." A sunset, a letter from a friend, the fields of hay shining in the rising sun, the smell of jasmine, the singular look of a loved one, a soup bubbling on a wood stove, the autumn trees, bathing under a waterfall, hands holding you up, the hug of a child—there have been many moments in my life of such beauty that I tell myself: "It was worth having lived my whole life just to have been able to live this moment." There are passing moments that justify a whole life.

Suddenly I understood that the pain of the interrupted sonata is owed to the fact that we live under the spell of time. We think life is a sonata that begins at birth and should end with old age. But this is wrong. We live in time, it is quite true. But it's eternity that gives meaning to life.

Eternity isn't time without end. Time without end is intolerable. Have you ever imagined a song without end, a kiss without end, a book without end? All that is beautiful must end. All that is beautiful must die. Beauty and death always walk hand in hand.

Eternity is completed time, that time about which people say, "It was worth it." Neither evolution nor transformation is necessary. Time is complete and happiness is total. Of course this, according to

Guimarães Rosa, only happens at rare moments of distraction. It doesn't matter. If it happened, it became eternal. Contrary to the "never again" of chronological time, this moment is destined to "for all of always."

So I understood that life is not a sonata that, to fulfill its beauty, must be played to the end. It let me understand, to the contrary, that life is an album of mini-sonatas. Each moment of beauty lived and loved, ephemeral though it may be, is a complete experience that is destined to eternity. One singular moment of beauty and love justifies an entire life.

VII
Presto-Allegro Assai

with the vibrato
of the Ninth Symphony of
L. van Beethoven

Rubem Alves

I Am Going To Plant a Tree

A long time ago—exactly eleven years ago, on December 1987—I wrote the following:

> *I am going to plant a tree. It will be my gesture of hope. A broad crown, friendly shade, strong branches, kids on a swing, lots of plump fruit, songbirds flying around. But most important of all, it will have to grow slowly, very slowly. So slowly that I will never sit in its shade… The first person to plant a tree in whose shade he or she would never sit was the first to speak the name of the Messiah.*

Camus, my dear brother Camus, one lazy, twilight afternoon—lazy times are the most creative, times when the gods open our eyes so we can see what we've never seen—wrote the following in his diary: "During the day the flight of birds seems without destination; at night they always aim for a certain place. They fly somewhere. Maybe it's that way in the nighttime of life..."

Yep. When we're young, we fly in all directions. Our hopes are many, and we don't want to miss any of them. When we're older, we better understand that one is worth more than many. It's like in that parable Jesus told, about a man who, all of a sudden, found a wonderful jewel. Fascinated by it, he went and sold everything he owned so he could buy it. "Purity of heart," said Kierkegaard, "is to wish for just one thing." Whoever has many hopes is a pile of broken glass. Whoever has just a single hope is a stained glass window of a cathedral.

My stained glass window is still that scene: that tree and the kids on a swing. It's a heavenly scene. I'm happy just to imagine the happiness of the children. In old age, our eating habits change. It's enough for us to each day to eat the image of happiness in our grandchildren...

Emily Dickenson wrote this delicious little poem:

> *To make a prairie it takes a clover and one bee,*
> *One clover, and a bee.*
> *And revery.*
> *The revery alone will do,*
> *if bees are few.*

So beautiful and such a lie! This is one flaw in poets. Lacking solid food, they often lie and make up a story (as Fernando Pessoa confessed, "the poet is a pretender"...) so their lies become food. That was the case of solitary Emily, who fed herself on virtual prairies. I could even eat food like that if I were the only person involved. But my grandchildren are not virtual. They are children of flesh and bone. For them, fantasies do not suffice. So for me, the last line of the poem would have to be different: "But, if bees are few, *I need to call bees!*" How easy it would be if I had a magic flute, as in that story about the flutist in

Hamelin. I would play enchanting music, and the bees would follow me.

In that I have no flute, all I can do is the next best thing—try to be an educator. An educator is a person who, desiring a prairie, calls bees. Lacking a flute, he or she speaks, and with speech draws the world he or she loves. *An educator is a creator of worlds.* The educator's wish is to be a god because as a god, he or she could create, alone, his or her paradise. Saying the magic word would be enough to make the tree with the kids and swing appear. Not being gods—having only the "dream" of gods without having their "power"—all that's left is to go out into the world to talk about their dreams. The image of that flower in the field came to me, an image of a ball of white seeds. You give it a blow, and the seeds fly off like parachutes to be born far away, wherever the wind takes them. That's the educator—a ball of word-seeds where you find the dream they wish to plant.

Educator, ball of seeds: a species in extinction. What proliferates is professors specialized in teaching pieces and fragments. Every course is a fragment. In the service of science, there's no alternative because only pieces and fragments can be discussed with scientific objectivity.

But the trees, the swings, the kids don't live in the place where scientists research and teachers teach. Scientists and teachers live in the space of knowledge—which is very good and necessary. To plant a tree and make a swing, knowledge is necessary. But knowledge alone doesn't make anyone *wish* to plant a tree and hang a swing. For that, you need love. Worlds that are to be created, before they exist as reality, exist as fantasies of love.

My sadness has something to do with this fact: everything indicates that my dream will not be carried out. The bees are few, the raptors many. The prairies are being increasingly replaced by dead things. With deep sadness I read a prayer written almost a hundred years ago:

> *O God, we pray for those who will come after us,*
> *for our children and for all the lives that are being*

> *born now, pure and hopeful. We remember, with anguish, that they will live in the world that we are building for them. We are using up the world's resources with our greed, and they will suffer need because of this. We are poisoning the air of our world with our filth, and they will have to breathe it.* (Prayers for a Better World, *Paulus*)

I love waterfalls, trails through the woods, paths over mountains, rivers and their backwaters, the sea and beaches. But wherever man goes, there you find signs of his call to destruction and devastation. They don't go to the beach to hear the music of the sea. They go to the beach to socialize their insanity and agitation. They don't go to the woods and waterfalls to recuperate their lost harmony with nature. They go to woods and waterfalls to leave their trash and excrement. With the passing of the savage hordes (forgive me, savages! Savages are precisely those who no longer do that, for they are those who inhabit jungles and know how they are sacred. Hordes of *what*? I cannot find a word that describes the horror of human behavior in the face of nature.) They become witnesses of the disrespect of man for Mother Nature. What man is building as the future of their children and grandchildren isn't a paradise of trees and creeks but an electronic jungle of metal, cement, and trash.

E.e. Cummings said that "better worlds aren't made; they're born." Where are they born? Love is the only power from which things are born. Artists know this. And this is what I am looking for, as an educator. I want to teach love. If we don't love nature, there isn't the least possibility that it will end up preserved. I know this sounds mushy. Scientists of education will laugh at me—because what interests them is the transmission of knowledge. Researchers at universities prefer to write their articles for international magazines. I confess that, right now, this would not be a jewel for which I would sell everything, nor the direction of my twilight flight. The increase of knowledge doesn't excite me at the moment. We already know too much. If we use a hundredth of what we know, the world would be a wonderful place. What we lack isn't knowledge. It's love. That's why I'm an educator. I want companions for the job of planting trees and hanging swings...

Bovine Wisdom

Ideas are of two types. Those of the first type are birds that get snagged in traps that science calls "method." Whoever sets a methodological trap is looking for something. If I am looking for something, I should know beforehand what it should be. Otherwise I won't be able to recognize it, should I encounter it. In the methodological traps of science, unknown birds do not get snagged. These birds, before getting caught, have already been imagined. The imagining of the ways of the bird to be caught in the methodological traps has the name "hypothesis."

Those of the second type are birds that don't get caught in traps. Truth is, they can't be caught. They just come and land on your shoulder. Picasso said that he did not seek. He simply found. That is, he did not go out looking for something. He went out, and the "thing," unthought, suddenly showed up before him. These are the innovative ideas that open up new scenarios. There is no method for snagging them for the simple reason that they are not known to us. Their appearance always happens by surprise. That's why Nietzsche said that its appearance is always accompanied with a smile.

These ideas appear in unexpected situations. Archimedes was struggling to solve a problem that the king had given him, but to no avail. It was in a moment of relaxation, as he sank into a bathtub, that the solution appeared like a sudden revelation that had fallen from the sky. Legend has it that something similar happened to Newton, giving him an understanding of the law of universal gravity as it hit him for the first time, a law in the guise of an apple that fell from the branch of an apple tree, something he had seen happen countless times before. Kekulê was confounded by the problem of the structure of benzene. It is said that he solved the problem while looking at a smoke ring that came from his cigar. He noticed that the structure wasn't a long sausage but a snake biting its own tail.

Well something similar happened to me a few days ago. I was going down a narrow dirt road at night, playing around with common bird-ideas that I had caught in a trap, when I came upon a bunch of cows. I wasn't prepared for that. In that situation, the cows were, to me, just a gathering of ruminant quadrupeds that were blocking my car. I honked. To no avail. It was as if I hadn't done anything. The bovine intelligence did not understand my attempts at communication. So I carefully and slowly moved my bumper up against their legs. Then they understood and started opening a way, lazily, against their will, without altering for a moment the rhythm of their ruminant chewing. I thought that I had found the most perfect incarnation of stoic wisdom that I had ever seen, a living example of ataraxia, absolute indifference to outside disturbance. Stupidity is often a source of tranquility and virtues. As I passed the last cow, this one, in a supreme act of displeasure, produced a *quantum* of fecal dough. When it smacked to the ground with a sound characteristic of the stuff, it launched an asteroid of green feces into my beard.

"Stupid animals," I thought indignantly. Really stupid. Only good for milk and meat. I've already seen, in a circus, a dog, horse, tiger, lion, bear, monkey, elephant, seal, all doing cute little things. Have you ever seen a cow in a circus show? Never. They're too dumb and dull-witted. It got me thinking about the extent of a cow's intelligence. It must be very small. Then I thought that despite this, they have survived for millennia. They must have another intelligence, an enormous one not found anywhere where we commonly put them. And I came to understand that this fantastic, incredible, monumental wisdom resides within those paunchy, lazy bodies. Cows are structural wonders, biochemical mills that make everything out of air, water, and grass, perfect machines for the transformation of energy. All of this know-how is there, silent and active, in the body of cows. Their heads don't know any of this. Her head doesn't know anything about the gestation of calves or the production of milk. Nevertheless, they give birth to calves and produce milk.

So then I thought about Descartes, who said that famous sentence, "I think, therefore I am." That is, he placed the *being* of a person inside thought. Imagine if there were a philosopher cow (in the world of imagination, anything is possible) and that she had read Descartes. She would have been hit with a smile attack. "Oh! If the *being* of a cow was in thought, we would have ceased to exist long ago. Our *being* is found somewhere else..."

Now, if this can't be said of cows, it can't be said of humans, either. Our *being* isn't found in our thought. Our body knows infinitely more than our head. The body is wise, even without thinking about its wisdom. That's the word of a psychoanalyst. I also say that the word *unconscious* is only the word for the thoughts that reside in the body, without their head knowing about them.

What separates us from animals is that the thoughts that live in our heads have wandered off to proliferate, multiply, and grow. This had unarguable advantages because it was thanks to our thoughts in our heads that the human world constructed itself. Philosophy, science, technology. (When we speak of technology, people generally think of big wonderworks. But technology is the wheel, the mouse trap, the wedge, string, knife, pot...simple day-to-day things.)

These thoughts grew so much that they started to clog up the wisdom of the body. Knowledge went on growing, sedimenting layer on layer, until there came a moment when we forgot the wisdom that lives in the body. Then we went into a condition worse than that of cows. Because cows never forgot the wisdom of their bodies. People with knowledge are often the enemy of wisdom. I know erudite idiots. T.S. Eliot was astonished by this and asked himself, "Where is the *wisdom* that we lost in *knowledge*? Where is the *knowledge* that we lost in *information*?" Manuel de Barros, without Eliot's aristocratic subtlety, said it more straightforward: "Whoever accumulates information loses the virtue of divining: *div-*

inare. The wise divine. The wise one is the one who divines."

I am afraid that the many people of knowledge do this with us. Unfortunately, schools, so preoccupied with developing tests of the knowledge that resides in the head, have no notion of the wisdom that lives in the body.

Concerto for Body and Soul

On Optimism and Hope

It was the year 1898. Everyone was talking about the new century that was approaching, the twentieth century. There were more than enough reasons for hope. Humanity was ready to see what had been prophesied 200 years before.

> *Whatever the beginning of this world was, it is certain that the end will be glorious and heavenly… Mankind will make this world more and more comfortable and will prolong his existence and will become more and more happy.*

There was nothing wondrous about that prophesy. It was simply enunciating what everyone believed. They believed that the history of humanity was a long epic journey that began millions of years ago. Its beginning was insignificant. The insignificant is a seed. No one suspects the beauty or the size of the tree that it contains. Smaller than an amoeba. But time does its work. New forms of life were born of each other, dramatically, some disappearing, others surviving, until at last, at the end of this torturous process there would be a wonderful fruit: beautiful, good, intelligent mankind. The seed will have turned into a tree with a lovely green canopy covered with flowers and fruit. Many fruits had already ripened, and men had savored their taste. But the great harvest was yet to come. The great harvest would be the twentieth century.

On the occasion of the seventieth birthday of the poet Walt Whitman, Mark Twain wrote him a wonderful letter, the greatest document of optimism that I know of:

> *You have lived the seventy years which are greatest in the world's history & richest in benefit & advancement to its peoples. These seventy years have*

done much more to widen the interval between man & the other animals than was accomplished by any five centuries which preceded them. What great births you have witnessed! The steam press, the steamship, the steel ship, the railroad, the perfected cotton-gin, the telegraph, the phonograph, the photograph, photo-gravure, the electrotype, the gaslight, the electric light, the sewing machine, & the amazing, infinitely varied & innumerable products of coal tar, those latest & strangest marvels of a marvelous age. And you have seen even greater births than these; for you have seen the application of anesthesia to surgery-practice, whereby the ancient dominion of pain, which began with the first created life, came to an end in this earth forever; you have seen the slave set free, you have seen the monarchy banished from France, & reduced in England to a machine which makes an imposing show of diligence & attention to business, but isn't connected with the works. Yes, you have indeed seen much — but tarry yet a while, for the greatest is yet to come. Wait thirty years, & then look out over the earth! You shall see marvels upon marvels added to these whose nativity you have witnessed; & conspicuous above them you shall see their formidable Result—Man at almost his full stature at last! — & still growing, visibly growing while you look. In that day, who that hath a throne, or a gilded privilege not attainable by his neighbor, let him procure his slippers & get ready to dance, for there is going to be music. Abide, & see these things! Thirty of us who honor & love you, offer the opportunity: We have among us 600 years, good & sound, left in the bank of life. Take 30 of them — the richest birthday gift ever offered to a poet in this world — & sit down & wait. Wait till you see that great figure appear, & catch the far glint of the sun upon his banner; then you may depart satisfied, as knowing you have seen him for whom the earth was made, & that he will proclaim that human wheat is worth more than human tares, & proceed to organize human values on that basis.

This grandiose idea of progress had appeared, perhaps for the first time and in a religious form, in the thought of Joaquim de Fiori, a heretic monk who died around the year 1200. His heresy was this: the theology of the Middle Ages saw the universe as similar to a Gothic Cathedral—a vertical hierarchy of incomparable structural beauty, ready right out of God's hands, unmovable in time. In it, all movements were vertical. Ascendant movements reached for the sky, and descendent movements went in the direction of Hell. The universe was only a physical scenario for the great spiritual drama of salvation. The destiny of mankind, upon salvation, was above, on high, the place where God lived. Joaquim de Fiori painted a new world. Heaven wasn't on high. It was found in the future. Space would be transformed by the power of time. It was like a woman in the pangs of childbirth. History is the movement of the universe impregnated by God. First the Father. Then, the Son. Finally, the Holy Spirit. At last, the birth. Paradise would be born.

The Gothic medieval cathedral universe collapsed. So did the universe of Joaquim de Fiori, who had been driven by the power of God. Scientists examined the skies and found them full of stars and marvelous galaxies—but no sign of God's living quarters. God was evicted from his mansion on high. But, without noticing, mankind had brought him to Earth and made him live in another place, a place with another name. They put him to live right inside history and gave him the name Reason. Reason is the divine power that, inside history, and in spite of the errors and wrong turns of mankind, let mankind reach a final paradise. How can one not be optimistic to live in such a universe?

Marxism was the greatest expression of that religion without God. It sought to provide scientific bases to optimism. Therein lies its fascination. Who doesn't wish for happy certainties about the future? I would like the certainty that my grandchildren will live in a heavenly world. That is precisely what Marxism proclaimed: through the process of torturous and suffering struggles, somewhat like that described by Darwin, mankind would arrive in a world without conflict in which the contradictory would be reconciled, and it would be possible to live in fraternity and justice, and mankind would finally be able to find happiness. It was a secular version of the messianic visions of the prophet Isaiah—the lion eating hay with the ox, the children playing with venomous snakes.

At the end of the nineteenth century, the wonderful conquests of science and technology, the rational ordering of politics through democratic processes, the development of education—all this was evidence that made unlimited optimism inevitable. It's a world wonderfully depicted by the impressionistic painters Monet and Renoir—the innocence, the joy, the colorful reflexes of nature, the lightness, the freedom from worry. The paintings of Renoir and Monet are manifestations of that happy soul.

But this marvelous journey toward the Holy City, shimmering on the heights of the mountain, hit a curve in the road, revealed another fate: barbarianism. Mankind became the owner of a body of scientific knowledge infinitely superior to all the knowledge accumulated in the past. The fragility of education was revealed. Knowledge and science were producing neither wisdom nor goodness. It was this man of education and scientific knowledge who produced two world wars. Along came Nazi extermination camps, communism, the creation of monstrous and lethal weapons, previously unimaginable wealth alongside millions dying of hunger, massacres, the destruction of nature and the sources of life, infernal cities, violence, terrorism with arms produced and sold by companies that generated progress.

And suddenly the wonderful Result announced by Mark Twain appeared in the monstrous form of paintings by Dali and Picasso—the demonic side of mankind announced by psychoanalysis.

Today there are no reasons for optimism. Today only hope is possible. Hope is the opposite of optimism. Optimism is when it's springtime outdoors, and springtime is born indoors. Hope is when it's absolutely dry outdoors, and springs continue to bubble in the heart. Camus knew what hope was. His words: "And in the middle of winter, I discovered that inside me was an invincible summer..." Optimism is joy "because of." It's a naturally human thing. Hope is joy "in spite of." It's a divine thing. Optimism has its roots in time. Hope has its roots in eternity. Optimism is fed by big things. Without them, it dies. Hope is fed with small things. In small things it blooms. Today, all we have as we enter the twentieth century is strawberries at the edge of the abyss, happiness without cause. The possibility of hope…

Acknowledgements

New London Librarium would like to thank Senior Editors Denise Dembinski and Ralph Hunter Cheney for scrutinizing every word and point of punctuation in this book. We also extend our gratitude to Raquel Alves, the Instituto Rubem Alves, and Editora Papirus for allowing us to bring the musings of Rubem Alves to the English-speaking world.

About Rubem Alves

Rubem Alves (1933–2014) was a theologian, philosopher, educator, psychoanalyst, and one of Brazil's most popular writers. Born in Boa Esperança, Minas Gerais, he went on to earn a Ph.D. from Princeton Theological Seminary. He also trained and practiced as a psychoanalyst. His most recent professorship was at the Universidade Estadual at Campinas in São-Paulo state. He is the author of hundreds of essays and 40 books on pedagogy, theology, philosophy, and life in general. His works have been published in 13 countries and translated into various languages. More information is available at the Instituto Rubem Alves in Campinas (www.rubemalves.com.br).

About the Translator

Glenn Alan Cheney is a translator, writer, and editor in Hanover, Conn. His more than 25 books explore myriad topics, including Brazil's Estrada Real and the Quilombo dos Palmares, nuns, Chernobyl, nuclear issues, the Pilgrims, Abraham Lincoln, Mahatma Gandhi, Central American insurrections, Amazonia, bees, cats, death and burial, the end of the world, incarceration, and Swaziland, as well as novels, stories, poems, and essays. He is the founder and managing editor of New London Librarium.

New London Librarium

New London Librarium is a small literary press in Hanover, Conn. that specializes in works that deserve publication but whose market would not justify publication by a larger house. Special series include art, Brazil, Catholic issues, controversial issues, fiction, and history. Many of its titles are translations of Brazilian classics. For more information and the catalog, see NLLibrarium.com.

www.ingramcontent.com/pod-product-compliance
Lightning Source LLC
Chambersburg PA
CBHW030331230426
43661CB00032B/1371/J